CALLED
TO SERVE

MINISTRY AND MINISTERS IN THE CHURCH

Michael Green

CHRISTIAN FOUNDATIONS

CALLED TO SERVE

Christian Foundations

A series edited by Philip E. Hughes

CALLED TO SERVE

MINISTRY AND MINISTERS IN THE CHURCH

by

MICHAEL GREEN

1344

Philadelphia
The Westminster Press

Library of Congress Catalog Card No. 65–16838

Published by The Westminster Press ®
Philadelphia, Pennsylvania

PRINTED IN THE UNITED STATES OF AMERICA

CONTENTS

The author wishes to express his warm gratitude to Mrs. U. Vessey for the trouble she has taken in typing the manuscript, to his wife, to the Rev. J. R. W. Stott, the Rev. Dr. J. I. Packer, and to several colleagues and students at the London College of Divinity for their helpful criticisms and suggestions.

CHRONOLOGICAL GUIDE

to some of the Patristic material mentioned in this book

Clement of Rome: wrote his letter to the Corinthians *c.* A.D. 96.

Ignatius: bishop of Antioch, wrote to several Asian Churches, and was martyred in Rome *c.* A.D. 107.

The Didache: a short early Christian treatise on morals and church practice. Although the author, date and place of origin are unknown, recent scholarship favours a date in the later first or early second century A.D.

Polycarp: bishop of Smyrna, wrote a letter to the Philippians, and was martyred in Smyrna A.D. 155.

Justin: a Christian philosopher and apologist, martyred *c.* A.D. 165 in Rome.

Hermas: an early second-century Roman writer.

Hegesippus: a Jewish Christian of the second century who wrote church history; known only in quotations.

Montanism: a prophetic movement led by Montanus and two prophetesses towards the end of the second century; it provided a serious challenge to catholic Christianity.

Clement of Alexandria: distinguished theologian and author, died *c.* A.D. 215.

Origen: succeeded Clement at Alexandria, died *c.* A.D. 254.

Tertullian: a Roman African lawyer and prolific author, died *c.* A.D. 220.

Cyprian: bishop of Carthage, died *c.* A.D. 258.

Pseudo-Clementines: writings of the second or third centuries A.D. wrongly ascribed to Clement of Rome.

Eusebius: bishop of Caesarea and 'father of church history', died *c.* A.D. 340.

Apostolic Constitutions: a manual of church order of the fourth century, but incorporating earlier material.

Epiphanius: bishop of Salamis and dogmatician, died A.D. 403.

Chrysostom: bishop of Constantinople and theologian, died
A.D. 407.
Jerome: ascetic and learned biblical scholar, died A.D. 420.
Augustine: bishop of Hippo, theologian, and author, died A.D.
430.

FOREWORD

CHRISTIAN FOUNDATIONS is a series of paperback books written by evangelical churchmen and designed to reaffirm the doctrine of the New Testament in the light of the past history, the present needs, and the future development of the Church. The series appears under the auspices of the Evangelical Fellowship in the Anglican Communion, and the authors are all members of that Communion. But their concern is for the whole Church, and not for just one portion of it. They have no desire to promote any kind of narrow denominationalism or to avoid involvement in the contemporary ecumenical debate. As the Archbishop of Sydney said in his Foreword to the British edition, 'these books have a truly catholic scope, and accordingly they can speak with clarity and also charity to those on either side of Anglicanism, and indeed, to many who at present are outside the fellowship of Christian believers'. The unity that the authors covet for the Church is unity in the truth—not unity at any price, least of all at the price of dispensing with the foundations of the faith which has been once delivered to the Church. They are convinced that, as evangelicals, they have a full and essential contribution to make, especially in advocating the recovery of the dynamic witness, the apostolic teaching, the fellowship in worship, and the victorious living of the New Testament; for these, they believe, are the vital principles of Christian unity in faith and action.

In view of the fact that some of the books deal with controversial issues, it is not expected that there will always be agreement with each particular position that may be propounded; but it is hoped that the books will be received in the spirit in which they are offered, which is not one of contention but of goodwill and reasonableness. The authors only ask for an unprejudiced hearing. Naturally they seek to persuade; yet where they fail to do that, they will be content if any discussion that arises is conducted before the bar of the scriptural revelation. They wish that all together, however different their viewpoints, might follow the example of the Christians in Beroea who searched the Scriptures to see whether the things they had been told were true (Acts 17:10 f.). To do just this could in itself hardly fail to have the effect of bringing us all closer together.

In current ecumenical discussion and negotiation it is over differing interpretations of the doctrine of the ministry that there is the sharpest disagreement. In fact, it may be said that the greatest single obstacle in the way of Church reunion is the narrow view held by some of episcopacy as belonging in some way to the *esse* of the Church and alone guaranteeing the transmission of valid ministerial orders and sacramental grace. This attitude reflects unfavourably, of course, on those Churches whose ministries are of the non-episcopal kind. In a country like the United States of America, for example, it virtually unchurches those denominations—Presbyterian, Methodist, Baptist, Congregational, and so on—whose united membership forms a majority of the total Church membership in that land. Boldly and learnedly, Mr. Green seizes this theological nettle. He investigates the doctrine of the ministry in the New Testament, and as it developed in the subsequent centuries. He shows that classical Anglicanism regarded genuine apostolicity as consisting in faithfulness to the teaching of the apostles and not in some particular form of Church order, and that consequently it did not entertain doubts concerning the validity of the ministries and sacraments of non-episcopal Churches which were of the same persuasion in matters of faith and doctrine.

But important and necessary as this undoubtedly is, Mr. Green is intent on reminding us of another factor that, as the very name ministry itself implies, is essential to a right understanding of the ministerial functions, namely, that it is a vocation to service: the Christian minister is called to be a servant, not a Lord; to be humble, not arrogant; to magnify his Master, not himself. Clericalism in one form or another is all too prevalent in the Church today. This book points us clearly to the antidote.

P. E. H.

Note: In this book and in others of the CHRISTIAN FOUNDATION series, mention of the 'Articles' in general, or of certain Articles in particular (for example, 'Article XI' or 'Article

XXXVII'), should be understood to refer to the Thirty-Nine Articles of Religion of the Church of England (1563). Parallels to many of the statements in these doctrinal formulae could have been cited, of course, from sixteenth-century Reformation confessions such as the Augsburg Confession (1530), the Second Helvetic Confession (1566), and the Scottish Confession (1560), and from later statements such as the Westminster Confession (1647).

Details of those books which are mentioned but not described in the footnotes will be found in the Select Bibliography.

CHAPTER I

THE MINISTRY OF JESUS

JESUS' whole ministry was one of service. This is clearly shown both by the general tenor of the Gospel narrative, and by many specific utterances. Thus, when approaching the climax of His ministry at Jerusalem, Jesus declared: 'The Son of Man came not to be served but to serve, and to give His life as a ransom for many' (Mk. 10: 45). He made it very clear, in the verses immediately preceding these words, that service was to be the hallmark of all Christian ministry. In contrast to worldly rulers, preoccupied with status and authority, 'It shall not', He said, 'be so among you; but whoever would be great among you must be your servant, and whoever would be first among you must be slave of all.'

This lesson of the royalty of service must have been indelibly imprinted on the minds of the disciples by what happened at the Last Supper. In the Middle East, feet quickly get hot and dusty, and it was the job of the household slave to wash them. At the Last Supper there was no household slave. None of the apostles was willing to lose face by doing the slave's job, so they ate with unwashed feet. We can imagine their amazement when Jesus 'rose from supper, laid aside His garments, and girded Himself with a towel . . . and began to wash the disciples' feet' (Jn. 13: 4, 5). He was introducing them to a revolutionary idea of greatness—measured in terms of service. Relentlessly the moral is pressed home. 'Do you know what I have done to you? You call me Teacher and Lord; and you are right, for so I am. If I then, your Lord and Teacher, have washed your feet, you also ought to wash one another's feet. For I have given you an example, that you also should do as I have done to you. Truly, truly, I say to you, a servant is not greater than his master; nor is He who is sent greater than He who sent Him. If you know these things, blessed are you if you do them' (13: 12–17).

There is, I think, a hint in St. Luke's account that this action of Jesus arose out of a quarrel among the disciples over precedence and status. Although he does not record the actual footwashing, Luke does tell us of this devastating question which Jesus asked them at this meal: 'Which is the greater, one who sits at table, or one who serves? Is it not the one who sits at table? But I am among you as one who serves.' Once more Jesus makes it crystal-clear that what is true of Him, must be true of His disciples: 'The kings of the Gentiles exercise lordship over them . . . but not so with you; rather let the greatest among you become as the youngest, and the leader as one who serves' (Lk. 22: 24–27).

The Christian Church has found this a very hard lesson to learn. Almost all consideration of different types of Christian ministries begins with a discussion of the validity of the orders in question, of their regularity, their authentication, their apostolicity. That is very natural. It is the way of the world. But it is not the way of Jesus Christ. He saw ministry not in terms of status but rather in terms of function. The pattern for Christian ministry which He set was one of service. Of course, the very word 'ministry' means 'service'. But for Jesus this was no idle euphemism. It is no accident that the term 'ministry' is used to describe the whole of His public life and work. He was supremely, and in everything, the Servant of the Lord. This was His glory; He looked for no other. And so it must be with any ministry which claims to be truly Christian.

A. JESUS, THE SERVANT

If we ask how Jesus came to think of Himself in this light, the answer is plain enough. He found it in His Bible, and in particular in Isaiah 40–55. Here it is made very plain that the whole nation of Israel is called to be the Servant of the Lord; service is the corollary of election (Is. 41: 8–20). The particular elements of service that are asked of the nation of Israel are obedience (Is. 44: 1, cf. 65: 12), witness (43: 12) and endurance (43: 1–6). But the nation refused to obey, recoiled from suffering, and instead of witnessing to the Lord gave way to idolatry. And so the task of the servant of the Lord devolves on a faithful remnant within Israel, who accept its implications. In the four Servant Songs of Isaiah (42: 1–4, 49: 1–6, 50: 4–7 and 52: 13–53: 12) the great themes are obedience, witness and endurance. The Servant is utterly obedient to God's voice (42: 1, 50: 4, 5), witnesses both to the lapsed among Israel and to the Gentiles (49: 6), and suffers ignominy and pain

(50: 5, 6). Indeed, although innocent, he bears the sins of the people (53: 6, 11, 12), and God will accept his sacrifice, and vindicate his cause (53: 10-12).

We may never know just how the prophet thought his words would be fulfilled, but it is certain that Jesus saw in them the foreshadowing of His own ministry, at any rate after the Baptism, when the voice from heaven addressed Him as 'My beloved Son, in whom I am well pleased' (Mk. 1: 11). These words are a composite quotation from Psalm 2: 7 and Isaiah 42: 1. Jesus the Messianic *Son* is hailed as the *Servant* of the Lord in whom His soul delights. The point is made equally emphatically at the outset of St. John's Gospel where Jesus is greeted by the Baptist as 'the Lamb of God who takes away the sin of the world' (Jn. 1: 29, 36). This title would, of course, have taken his Jewish hearers back to the sacrificial system they knew so well. But it would have done more. It would have pointed them to the Suffering Servant of Isaiah 53, for *talya*, the Aramaic word for 'lamb', is also the word for 'servant'.

The three themes of utter obedience, fearless witness and innocent suffering, which marked the Old Testament conception of the Servant of the Lord, run through the ministry of Jesus. And so, when at Caesarea Philippi Peter makes his great confession that Jesus is the Messiah, the long awaited deliverer of Jewish expectation, Jesus 'charged them to tell no one about Him' (Mk. 8: 30). If they were thinking in terms of status and position they were entirely missing the point. So Jesus reinterpreted Peter's confession. He would not allow the term 'Christ' (or 'Messiah'), which suggested earthly pomp and military might. Instead, He joined together two utterly diverse concepts, and in effect asked Peter to see Him in terms of them. 'He began to teach them that the *Son of Man* must *suffer* many things and be rejected . . .' Professor Cullmann is not exaggerating when he says: ' "Son of Man" represents the highest conceivable declaration of exaltation in Judaism; *ebed Yahweh* (the Servant of the Lord) is the expression of the deepest humiliation. This is the unheard-of new act of Jesus, that He united these two apparently contradictory tasks in His self-consciousness, and that He expressed that union in His life and teaching.'[1]

The concept of the Servant was never far from Jesus' mind, as can be seen from a whole page full of references and allusions

[1] *The Christology of the New Testament*, S.C.M., p. 161.

gathered by Professor Jeremias.[2] Moreover, it is clear that this became the dominant theme towards the end of Jesus' ministry. By word (for example Lk. 22: 37) and deed (Jn. 13: 4 ff., Mt. 26: 28) Jesus demonstrated that He was fulfilling the task of the Servant to the bitter end. Peter understands this (I Pet. 2: 21 ff.), so does Paul (Phil. 2: 6, 7). Both of them, in fact, make specific reference to Isaiah 53. Two of the early speeches in Acts refer to Jesus as God's Servant (3: 13, 26, 4: 27, 30; so, too, 8: 32 f.), and there are other New Testament allusions, such as Romans 15: 7–12. Of course, this title gave way to others after His Resurrection, notably 'Lord'; but it cannot be denied that the pattern and the glory of His ministry was service. It was, therefore, entirely in character when Jesus knelt to wash the disciples' feet. The Servant of the Lord had shrunk from the nation of Israel, from the faithful remnant, to a single person who fully embodied it. Later, it was to expand again in His followers. They are called to serve.

B. THE CHURCH OF THE SERVANT

Jesus is *the* Servant. He is *our* Servant. No man can be a Christian, let alone a Christian minister, until he lets Jesus be his Servant. Peter discovered this, though at first he rejected the notion outright: 'You shall never wash my feet.' But Jesus replied: 'If I do not wash you, you have no part in me.' Peter learnt his lesson, of course, and his first Epistle is full of the theme of the Servant. 'Submit' is the word that comes again and again; it is applied to husbands and wives, to young and old, to slaves – and to Christian leaders. In I Peter 5: 5 he uses a rare word for '*Clothe yourselves*, all of you, with humility', which suggests he had in mind the way Jesus took a towel and girded Himself. It is Peter's way of saying that the Church is to be marked with this characteristic of Jesus. It must be the Church of the Servant. Christian life begins when we allow Jesus to be our Servant. It continues as, incorporated into Christ, we share the role of the Servant which He made so much His own. Of course, we cannot share the atoning work of the Servant. He, and He alone, took responsibility for the sins of the world. But we can and must make His pattern of

[2] *The Servant of God*, S.C.M., pp. 98 f. See Mark 9: 31; 10: 33; 10: 45; 14:21, 24, 41. It is interesting to see how Jesus, in Mark 10: 45, dramatically reverses the specific destiny of the Son of Man according to Daniel 7: 14. He does not come to be saved, but to save.

ministry our own. Indeed, He commissions us to do so. That is made very plain in the two mission charges, to the Twelve (Mk. 6: 7 ff.) and to the Seventy (Lk. 10: 1 ff.). We meet the same characteristics of service that we saw in Isaiah and in the ministry of Jesus. They are to obey the instructions of Jesus in going out on this mission; they are to bear witness to the break-in of the kingly rule of God, and to urge men to change their minds and accept it. They are to serve those to whom they go by healing and casting out demons. They must be prepared to face suffering and rejection. Their ministry, in fact, is an extension of their Master's. It is conceived in the same terms, whether it be the Twelve or the Seventy. For apostles and for Church alike the pattern is the same. On this passage T. W. Manson comments: 'They justify their existence and earn their keep by the service that they render'; and he concludes: 'In the Kingdom of God, service is not a stepping-stone to nobility: it *is* nobility, the only kind of nobility that is recognized.'[3]

As the counterpart of this, Jesus warns His disciples against that preoccupation with status and succession that bedevilled the Jewish rabbinical schools. 'They love the place of honour at feasts, and the best seats in the synagogues, and salutations in the market places, and being called "Rabbi" by men. But you are not to be called "Rabbi", for you have one teacher, and you are all brethren. And call no man your "Father" on earth, for you have one Father, who is in heaven. Neither be called "Masters", for you have one Master, the Christ. He who is greatest among you shall be your servant' (Mt. 23: 6–11).

Such is the pattern for ministry set by Jesus. And He was the One who 'taught with authority and not as the scribes' (Mk. 1: 22), the One to whom 'all authority in heaven and earth' had been committed (Mt. 28: 18). It was the Christ, the Son of God, the Son of Man, who took upon Him the form of the Servant. He had irrefragable credentials had He wished to rely on status and authority. But He resolutely turned His back on any such suggestion. To Him the authority of the Servant lay simply in the fact of His service. The divine call, the divine equipment with the Holy Spirit, were demonstrated by obedience, by faithful witness, by patient endurance. These, and not some ecclesiastical counterpart to Gentile hierarchy (Lk. 22: 25) or Jewish succession (Mt. 23: 7, 8),

[3] *The Church's Ministry*, Hodder & Stoughton, p. 27.

were to be the authenticating marks of the Christian ministry.

When we reflect on the history of the Church, are we not bound to confess that she has failed to follow the example of her Founder? All too often she has worn the robes of the ruler, not the apron of the servant. Even in our own day it can hardly be said that the 'brand-image' of the Church is of a society united in love for Jesus, and devoted to selfless service of others.

If the Church as a whole has failed, the ministry has failed even more signally, to exhibit the character of the Servant. Even when we leave the past out of account, where pope and pastor, bishop and minister, priest and synod have all alike at times domineered over those in their charge instead of being examples to the flock (I Pet. 5: 3), the present is nothing to be proud about. Does the vicar give the impression of being the servant of his people? Does he not rather behave, as too often the missionary has behaved, like a little tin god, loving to be recognized and looked up to, anxious that nothing shall go on in his parish without his personal supervision? Is it not an astonishing reversal of the pattern left by Jesus when a bishop, a chief pastor of the flock, is glad to be called 'My Lord'?[4] Even today, in the ecumenical debate, *does* the ministry seek to commend itself by the marks of the Servant, or are not the issues quite different? When Rome insists on submission to the Roman pontiff as 'altogether necessary to salvation for every human creature' (the Bull *Unam Sanctam*). when the Anglican Communion insists on episcopacy as a *sine qua non* for reunion — is this the way of Jesus?

The question is vital and urgent. It is a nettle that must be firmly grasped. In England today there is an increasing unwillingness on the part of young people to accept authoritarian or traditional pronouncements on either doctrine or ethics. In the ecumenical field, greater *rapprochement* is threatened by heavily entrenched doctrines of the ministry which appear to

---

[4] One cannot help feeling that the whole gamut of ecclesiastical courtesy titles, 'the Venerable', 'the Very Reverend', 'the Most Reverend' and so on, are a hindrance rather than a help in the work of the ministry. They tend to build an invisible wall between their bearer and the world at large; much more important, they tend to make him just a little proud, just a little pleased with himself, just a little further removed than he was before from the role of the Servant.

be entirely uninfluenced by the example and precept of Jesus; while in almost every diocese in the churches of Asia and Africa there is a real desire for help from the older churches, *provided that* such new-style missionaries come, like their Master, 'not to be served but to serve'. Unless more than lip service is paid to this pattern of the Servant, the prospects of advance in any of these three fields is lamentably small.

CHAPTER TWO

THE MINISTRY OF THE EARLY CHURCH

DID the early Church follow up the ideals of service laid down by Jesus? In order to answer this question we shall examine first the ministry of all Christians as we find it in the New Testament, then the ministry in the specialized sense, and finally their relationship to one another.

A. THE MINISTRY OF ALL CHRISTIANS

There is no suggestion in the New Testament that one could possibly be a Christian without having a call to some form of ministry within the Church. The Christian is indeed 'saved to serve'. St. Paul, for one, could never forget that the voice of the ascended Christ at his conversion had said: 'Rise and stand upon your feet; for I have appeared to you for this purpose, to appoint you *to serve and to bear witness*' (Acts 26 : 16). It is hardly surprising, therefore, that the whole point of his argument in Romans 12 and I Corinthians 12 is that every member of the Christian body has his part to play in the service of God. He knew that ministry is the inalienable duty and privilege of every Christian. We, on the contrary, have so lost this conception of the universal requirement of Christians to serve their Lord, that we tend to understand ministry not in its New Testament sense of service, but of communication, administration. So anxious are we to transfer the plain duty of all to the sole responsibility of a church official!

Three words in particular are used to describe the devoted service of the man who knows himself to be forgiven.

1. The first is *doulos*. It means, quite baldly, bondslave. And it comes scores of times in the New Testament. It was a word which Paul sometimes used of his relation to his converts (1 Cor. 9: 19 f., 2 Cor. 4: 5), but most frequently of his own relation to Jesus. He was the 'bondslave of Jesus Christ' (Rom. 1: 1, etc.). He spoke of wearing the chain of a slave (II Tim. 1: 16), of being branded with the marks of a slave (Gal. 6: 17). He saw such dedication to Jesus as the only

fitting response of the redeemed. 'You are not your own,' he writes, 'you were bought with a price' (I Cor. 6: 19, 20). Peter makes the same plea for utter obedience to God, on precisely the same grounds: 'You know that you were ransomed ... with the precious blood of Christ' (I Pet. 1: 14–19); and he describes those who do not give God this service as 'denying the Master who bought them' (II Pet. 2: 1).

This metaphor of the slave was particularly relevant in the first century. The Roman slave belong entirely to his master. He had no rights at law, and could demand no privileges, though often, of course, under a kind master he would get excellent treatment. His money, his time, his future, his marriage were all, strictly speaking, at the disposal of his master. That is what it meant to be a slave. And that is the metaphor which the New Testament writers deliberately took over.

Peter and Paul apply it to themselves, apostles though they were; James and Jude, though, it would seem, blood half-brothers of Jesus (Mt. 13: 55), delight to call themselves His *douloi* (Jas. 1: 1, Jude 1: 1). It is, in fact, a characteristic description of Christians (Rev. 1: 1, I Pet. 2: 16). Could anything show more graphically their loving devotion and total dedication to Christ? Should this not shame into silence our arguments about the status and validity of ministries? The highest ministry of all is open to all—to be bondslaves of Jesus Christ.

2. The second word often used of Christian service is *leitourgos*, whence we derive our term 'liturgy'. If *doulos* speaks particularly of Christian devotion to Christ, *leitourgos* speaks of Christian worship of God. This is the word used of the angels in heaven (Heb. 1: 14) and of men on earth (for example Lk. 1: 23) as they ascribe worship to God and place themselves at His disposal for service (Acts 13: 1 ff.).

Sometimes the Jewish background of the term is uppermost, as in the Epistle to the Hebrews, where it is made very plain that the Old Testament priestly offerings, though ineffectual in themselves, are filled with meaning when seen in the light of Christ's work. They are, as it were 'fulfilled' in the self-offering of Jesus (8: 2, 6; 9: 21; 10: 11).

On the other hand it is from the imagery of pagan worship that Paul draws when he calls the faith of the Philippians a 'liturgy' (Phil. 2: 17). Similarly when state officials administer justice with a due sense of what they are doing, they can be described as 'ministers' of God (Rom. 13: 6).

More than once sacrificial Christian giving is described in this way; when Gentile churches make a collection for impoverished Jewish Christians (II Cor. 9: 12; Rom. 15: 27), this is *leitourgia*, a practical outworking of their genuine worship of God—nothing less would have induced them to do it! And for Epaphras to give himself, for the Lord's sake, to the service of Paul, was no less worthy of the name (Phil. 2: 30). Finally, when Paul, by God's enabling, preaches the Gospel to the heathen, this too is *leitourgia* (Rom. 15: 16) because, through it, converts are 'offered' to God. In short, this word speaks of the service of God in worship and in work. Once again, it is brought before us as the duty of every Christian, and not something which can be restricted or delegated to a special class within the Church.

3. The third and most common word is *diakonos*, from which our term 'deacon' is derived. Like the others, it is applied to all and sundry in the Christian Church. Jesus and the apostles are given this title, and it is used of the humblest believer. It refers particularly to service to others, often menial service at that. The varieties of service included in the term are vast. In Acts 6, for instance, the apostles were administering the Word of God to the people; the Seven were administering food. Both are called *diakonia* (Acts 6: 1, 4). The New Testament does not make our false distinction between the sacred and the secular. The whole of life is seen as belonging to God. The Christian's service to others must be done in the light of his relationship to God. The Church was very conscious, in these early days, that it was commissioned to carry on the work of the Servant.

We find the word used in I Corinthians 16: 15 of what we would call specific church work. It is no less appropriate to the personal service rendered by Timothy and Erastus to Paul (Acts 19: 22)—including, no doubt, taking down his letters and cooking his meals! Prison visiting is given this honourable title in Philemon 13, and so is evangelistic preaching in Acts 20: 24. *Diakonia*, in short, belonged to the whole Church and to every member of it. No service was regarded as too menial or too exacting if only it would commend the Gospel of the grace of God. No one in the early Church would have quarrelled with Paul's statement: 'What we preach is not ourselves, but Jesus Christ as Lord, with ourselves your servants for Jesus' sake' (II Cor. 4: 5).

As Emil Brunner puts it: 'One thing is supremely important; that *all* minister, and that nowhere is to be perceived a separation or even merely a distinction between those who do and those who do not minister, between the active and the passive members of the body, between those who give and those who receive. There exists in the *Ecclesia* a universal duty and right of service, a universal readiness to serve, and at the same time the greatest possible differentiation of functions.'[1]

If then ministry of this sort, comprising devotion to Christ, worship of God, and service of others, must be the hallmark of every Christian, it must in greater measure characterize their leaders. This, as we have already seen, St. Peter is at pains to point out (I Pet. 5: 1–5). So is St. Paul: I Corinthians 4 is a case in point. He begins this chapter of rebuke to the proud, self-sufficient Corinthians by saying (v. 1): 'This is how one should regard us, as servants of Christ and stewards of the mysteries of God.' He goes on to contrast his own attitude with theirs (vv. 9–13); unlike them he gladly embraces the life of hardship, suffering and ignominy that goes with the loyal following of the Suffering Servant. He sees himself, to quote one of the pope's most noble (though not always most descriptive) titles, as *Servus Servorum Dei*, 'servant of the servants of God'.

B. THE SPECIALIZED MINISTRY

1. *Various Ministries within the Church*

The fact that service is to be the mark of all Christians, not merely of a ministerial *élite*, does not dispense with the need for specialization within the Christian community. St. Paul sees the Church as 'the Body of Christ'. That is to say, she is the agent of His purposes, the bearer of His life in the world. Christians are like members within the human body; they have different functions, offer different types of service to the whole Body, while they share the same life and belong together. Romans 12: 4–8 urges Christians to discover and make the most of their particular gift for the good of the whole. Paul mentions the *charismata* (God-given qualities) of prophecy, helpful service, teaching, encouragement, giving and leadership as examples of what he means, and love as the

[1] *The Misunderstanding of the Church*, p. 50.

bond which unites these diverse gifts into the harmonious unity of the Body. The function of leadership in the Church is just one among the other gifts of God to His Church.

I Corinthians 12 employs the same metaphor, and makes the added point that this differentiation of function within the Christian Body is the sovereign act of the Holy Trinity (vv. 4–6). God's purpose is that by mutual caring (v. 26) each member should use his proper gift for the edification and benefit of the whole Body. Paul concludes the chapter by showing them that different types of specialized ministry are God's gifts to His Church (v. 28). We may divide them, if we wish, into four rough groupings; ministry of the Word ('first apostles, second prophets, third teachers'); ministry of healing ('then workers of miracles, then healers'); ministry of administration and leadership ('helpers, administrators' — the word means literally governors or directors); and finally the ministry which the Corinthians — wrongly — prized most, that of ecstasy ('speakers in various kinds of tongues').

The Church is seen here as a living organism, in which there is this God-given differentiation of *function*. In fact, the contributions of various parts to the whole are described in this chapter by four interesting titles; they are *pneumatica*, functions assigned by the Holy Spirit; *charismata*, gracious opportunities of service together with a God-given ability to fulfil them; *energemata*, a word which draws attention to the active use of these opportunities or gifts; and *diakoniai*, a word which emphasizes that the purpose of it all is service to the Body as a whole.

Ephesians 4: 8–13 underlines this theme. Paul is speaking of the gifts of the ascended Christ to His Church: 'and His gifts were that some should be apostles, some prophets, some evangelists, some pastors and teachers, for the equipment of the saints for the work of ministry, for building up the body of Christ'. Once again we see a specialized ministry that is Christ's gift to His Church; the divine institution of the ministry could hardly be more strongly stated.

Furthermore, it can hardly be accidental that each of the ministries mentioned is a ministry of the Word. The apostles and prophets form Christ's foundation gift to the Church (Eph. 2: 20; 3: 5). The apostles, as we shall see later, occupied a unique and unrepeatable place in the history of the Church. They were chosen by Christ as witnesses of His saving work, who should proclaim it to the world (Acts 1: 8); men who could attest from personal experience the resurrection of Jesus (Acts 1: 22); eyewitnesses, in fact, whose testimony would enable those who had not been present to believe (Jn. 17: 20).

The prophets, too, belonged to the foundation layer of the Church. They were men, associated closely with the apostles, who spoke under the direct prompting of the Holy Spirit (for example Acts 11: 27 ff.; 21: 4, 9; Rev. 1: 3). They gradually died out after the end of the apostolic age. At all events, it became increasingly necessary to test their credentials (I Jn. 4: 1; Rev. 2: 20). In the *Didache* the genuine prophet is highly thought of, but men are well aware of counterfeits, and the shrewd advice is given that 'no prophet who orders a meal while "in the Spirit" shall eat of it; otherwise he is a false prophet' (11: 7)!

Evangelists and 'pastor-teachers', of course, have a continuing place in the Church for the spread and the deepening of Christian commitment. Very likely we should identify the latter with the teachers of I Corinthians 12: 28, and, indeed, with the presbyter/bishops of Acts 20 and the Pastoral Epistles; in both contexts great emphasis is placed upon their teaching the Word of God (Acts 20: 24–32; I Tim. 3: 2; Tit. 1: 9). This teaching function, we are told (Eph. 4: 11, 12), is the main purpose of the Christian ministry, which is that part within the Body expressly charged with the duty of equipping the 'saints' for their service in the world.

Now surely this is a very remarkable thing. We tend to assume, today, that the purpose of the ministry is primarily to do with the leading of public worship and the celebration of the sacraments. These functions are never once attributed to the ministry in the New Testament. The ministry there is concerned first and foremost with *didache*, the teaching of Christians so that they may the more effectively play their part in the world. That is to say that the ministry exists for the sake of the Church (and not *vice versa*, as is so often either taught or assumed), just as the Church in her turn exists for the sake of the world. The pattern of the Servant remains.

2. Clergy and Laity?

If we were to ask the New Testament writers, 'What is the difference between a clergyman and a layman?', they would not understand what we meant. For the Christianity of the New Testament does not know two classes of Christians, the professional and the amateur, so to speak. All Christians are the laity of God (I Pet. 2: 10 – Greek). All Christians, likewise, are ministers of God, and, as we have seen in these three Pauline passages, the tasks we consider perquisites of the clergy are mixed up quite naturally with others we would regard as lay. The New Testament knows nothing of a priestly caste. As Lightfoot put it in his celebrated Essay on *The Christian Ministry*,[2] 'the Christian ideal is a holy season extending the whole year round, a temple confined only by the limits of the habitable world, a priesthood coextensive with the human race' (p. 5).[3] He goes on to show how loyalty to this ideal did not, of course, preclude practical organization. Very soon we find Christian meetings for worship on the first day of the week (Acts 20: 7), fixed places for these meetings (for example Philem. 2), and various types of officers in the Church (for example Phil. 1: 1). This practical necessity did not however, prevent them from inveighing against those who 'observe days and months and seasons and years'. It did not stop them maintaining that 'God dwelleth not in temples made with hands.' 'It was,' Lightfoot continues, 'against the false principle that they waged war; the principle that ... gave absolute intrinsic value to subordinate aids and expedients ... (which) were no part of the essence of the Gospel; they must not be allowed to obscure the idea of Christian worship. So it was with the Christian priesthood. For communicating instruction and for preserving public order, for conducting public worship and dispensing social charities, it became necessary to appoint special officers. They are called stewards of God, servants or ministers of the Church, and the like; but the sacerdotal title is never once conferred upon them. The only priests under the Gospel, designated as such in the New Testament, are the saints, the members of the Christian brotherhood' (I Pet. 2: 5, 9; Rev. 1: 6, 5: 10, 20: 6).

That is why there is no hard and fast distinction between

---

[2] My quotations are from the edition published by Thynne & Jarvis (1927).

[3] He explains his meaning on p. 4, 'Every member of the human family was potentially a member of the Church, and, as such, a priest of God.'

clergy and laity in the New Testament. All alike are servants and ministers of God.

3. Ordination?

Nevertheless there is clear evidence of what we would call the ordained ministry in the New Testament period. We meet, as we shall see, bishops, presbyters, deacons, those that bear rule. There is evidence that in some cases at least they were set apart for this work with prayer and the laying on of hands. In Acts 14: 23 we read of Paul and Barnabas appointing elders in every church visited on the First Missionary Journey. The word used is *cheirotoneo*, which in later ecclesiastical usage means 'the laying on of hands'. However, in secular usage the word means simply 'to choose', 'select', 'appoint' (choice was originally made in the Greek city states by the people *raising their hand*), and this is the meaning of the word in its only other New Testament occurrence (II Cor. 8: 19), and in its three occurrences in Ignatius.[4] In the *Didache* (15: 1) the churches are told to select their own bishops and deacons, and *cheirotoneo* is the word used. This probably means that the congregation are to choose their leaders, though the possibility of their laying hands on them cannot be excluded. In Acts 6 it is uncertain whether the imposition of hands on the Seven is done by the multitude who selected them, or by the apostles before whom they were brought. In any case, Acts 6 looks not like an ordination but an *ad hoc* measure to relieve a particular situation, and must be regarded as of dubious relevance. The only other evidence on ordination in the New Testament concerns Timothy. Paul speaks (II Tim. 1: 6) of 'the gift of God which is within you through the laying on of my hands', which may, of course, refer to ordination; the context, however, does nothing to suggest it, and refers rather to the initial Christian experience of his mother and grandmother. It probably means, in Timothy's own case, the laying on of hands which accompanied baptism (Heb. 6: 1, 2; Acts 9: 17). In that case the only reference to Timothy's ordination, and the only certain reference to ordination in the New Testament would be in I Timothy 4: 14. This may be translated, with the R.S.V., as: 'Do not neglect the gift you have, which was given you by prophetic utterance when the elders laid their hands upon you.' Or it may mean, as Daube

[4] *Philad.* 10: 1; *Smyrn.* 11: 2; *Poly.* 7: 2.

and Jeremias[5] have suggested, 'when hands were laid upon you with the object of making you a presbyter'. In the former case we would have a corporate form of commissioning, as when the prophets and teachers at Antioch laid hands on Barnabas and Saul to separate them for the work of evangelism (Acts 13: 3). If, however, Daube's interpretation is right, it leaves open the question of who laid hands on Timothy—presumably the Apostle Paul, but we cannot say.

Despite the uncertainty about the imposition of hands, it seems reasonably clear that those who were seen to have the gift of leadership in the early Church were commissioned to perform this task in the congregation by some competent authority, either an apostle (as perhaps in the case of Timothy) or by an apostolic delegate (see Tit. 1: 5; ?I Tim. 5: 22), or by the elders already in office (?I Tim. 4: 14). There would thus be a public recognition by the Body of Christ of the gift of leadership imparted by God to a particular member, and a solemn commissioning of him, through their representatives, to exercise that gift for the benefit of the Body as a whole. In that sense, and that alone, is there any difference between 'clergy' and 'laity' in the New Testament. All too soon the 'double standard' (between the ordinary Christian and the particularly holy Christian), which has been so disastrous in the history of the Church, creeps in. Thus the *Didache* sees the 'ascetics' and those who can 'speak in the Spirit' as possessing *ipso facto*, a higher status than anyone else.[6] Already we are moving away from the primitive conviction that all Christians equally are called to serve.

C. THE RELATIONSHIP OF THE TWO

We have seen that in the New Testament *diakonia* is the prerogative of all. It is very interesting that this word should have been chosen to denote the particularly Christian conception of ministry. The term is scarcely used in the Greek Old Testament; it is not used of officers in pagan religious societies, and it is utterly incompatible with a hierarchical structure. This humble word, applied to all its ministries, reminds us that the Church of the New Testament renounces pomp and

[5] In *The New Testament and Rabbinic Judaism* (London, 1956), pp. 244 ff., and *Zeitschift für die neutestamentliche Wissenschaft* (1957), pp. 130 f.
[6] *Didache* 13: 3; 10: 7.

26

status for its officers, and acknowledges that the only greatness she knows is that of the Servant, the only specialized ministries those of special subordination. If we find ourselves thinking of the ministry in terms of office and status, of authority and validity, we go far astray from the thought of the Bible. Of course, ministry and authority are not mutually exclusive in the teaching of the apostles any more than we have seen them to be in that of Jesus. But the minister's authority does not demand obedience because of his position but because of his service. Thus Paul encourages the Christians at Thessalonica to 'respect those who labour among you and are over you in the Lord ... because of their *work*' (I Thess. 5: 12 f.). The proof that God has given a man the gift of ministry is seen when he exercises it for the benefit of the Church. The emphasis is less on office than on function. Thus leadership and teaching are the functions exercised by some within the Body (those whose *charisma* it is, I Cor. 12: 28), but nowhere do we meet the suggestion that clergy and laity (the very terms are not only anachronisms, but distortions of the New Testament position) have realms into which the other is not permitted to venture. Let us glance at three such realms normally reserved for the specialized ministry today.

Separate Spheres for 'Clergy' and 'Laity'?

1. Teaching is, as we have seen, an important function of the specialized ministry, and yet in the Corinthian church there was room for any member of the congregation to take part in the ministry of the Word if he had something to contribute (I Cor. 14: 26–29). Indeed, it is the fact that all take part in proclaiming the Word of God that convinces the unbeliever present that God is in their midst (24, 25).

2. Leading in worship may well have been a function of the specialized ministry, but there is no suggestion that it should be restricted to them. On the contrary, any member of the assembled congregation was free to contribute his piece of teaching, his piece of 'prophecy', his choice of a psalm, his speaking with tongues, provided all was done in an orderly and edifying manner (I Cor. 14: 26, 40). For centuries the element of *risk* in a vital, corporate worship of this kind has seemed too great; there is very little danger of disorder arising from excessive congregational participation in the older established churches of the world! There is an increasing

tendency, even among the Free Churches, towards a liturgical order of worship, and this was, of course, by no means entirely lacking in New Testament times.[7] But it is not these churches that are growing in a remarkable way today. Indeed, in most of them, as in the Church of England, these are days of retrenchment rather than advance. But when we turn to the Pentecostal churches, particularly in South America, we find a very different picture. They are growing at a spectacular rate, much faster than any other churches in the world today. The Elim Church, for instance, has only been in Brazil for nine years, but it has over 220 congregations — more than the Anglicans have built in 120 years. In São Paulo a vast church is under construction which will hold 25,000 — and it will be *filled*, probably nightly. The growth of the Pentecostal churches may be due to many causes, but not least is the fact that it is predominantly a *lay* church. They have, indeed, a ministry, but it is not a hierarchy. The ministers do a secular job, and they really seek to 'equip the saints for the work of service'. As a result every Christian bears constant witness to his faith in impromptu open-air meetings and in personal conversation with his friends. Every Christian is free to participate in the weekly — and nightly — meetings for worship. Doubtless these meetings are often somewhat disorderly, but they are *alive*, because the whole people of God take a real part. He would be a proud man who asserted that we have nothing to learn from them.

3. Or take the administration of the sacraments, which we tend to associate exclusively with the ordained ministry. It is significant that in the New Testament we are never told who should baptize and who should preside at the Lord's Supper. It apparently never occurred to the first generation of Christians that these actions hung together as a specific area into which no 'layman' might trespass. The word 'sacrament' is, of course, not found in the New Testament. It belongs to the heathen world of the Graeco-Roman Empire, and there is a good deal of truth in Brunner's contention that with Ignatius' emphasis on the eucharist as the *pharmakon athanasias*, 'the medicine for attaining immortality', and the bishop as the distributor of it,[8] we have passed from the New Testa-

[7] See Prof. C. F. D. Moule's *Worship in the New Testament*, Lutterworth Press, pp. 67 ff.
[8] *Eph.* 20: 2.

28

ment conception of the Church as a unity of persons redeemed by Christ, and united in the Holy Spirit, to a sub-personal conception of the Church as a collective whose unity flows from their common relationship to a thing, the sacrament.[9] Be that as it may, it seems reasonably clear that in the New Testament anyone may baptize. As E. Schweizer puts it most succinctly: 'The apostles do not as a rule baptize (Acts 10: 48; cf. 19: 5 beside 6a; I Cor. 1: 14–17); ordinary church members do (Acts 9: 18).'[10]

It seems likely, too, that anyone could preside at the Lord's Supper in the early days of the Church. Thus when there are abuses over the eucharist at Corinth, there is no one responsible person with whom Paul can expostulate. If in Acts 2: 46 the 'breaking of bread from house to house' refers to the holy communion, as most commentators think it does, then that settles the matter; for it is expressly stated that this is what the *converts* did. It was a 'lay' celebration. In the Pastoral Epistles Paul expresses great concern over church order, but he never suggests that the celebration of the eucharist or baptism is a function peculiar either to the presbyter-bishops whom Timothy and Titus are to ordain, or to the apostolic delegates themselves. Even as late as Justin (*Apology*, 1 : 65), in the middle of the second century, we find the celebrant referred to simply as *ho proestōs*, 'the president', presumably because, as in the *Didache*, it is not yet invariably the task of one particular official.

I am not in the least advocating indiscriminate celebrations of holy communion, but I believe the principle to be important; the New Testament knows of no special body to whom is entrusted the celebration of the sacraments, no priestly caste within the Christian Church. There may be something to be said for the practice of the Congregational Church in having a layman to preside at the eucharist once a year in order to make plain that the restriction of this function to the ordained ministry is a matter of order, not of doctrine. There is certainly a great deal to be said for celebration by a godly layman in areas such as isolated mission stations which would otherwise be deprived of the holy communion except for once or twice a year when a priest is available. In many places in the Far East pioneer missionary work is carried out

[9] *Op. cit.* chapters 7–10.
[10] *Church Order in the New Testament*, p. 186.

29

solely by women missionaries, while Christian men hold back from offering themselves for such arduous service.[11] The evangelization of primitive tribes is carried on by these dedicated women; the first baptisms are administered by them, the second by the missionary and the first believers jointly, and thereafter by the nationals themselves; the first eucharists are celebrated, probably in milk and rice, by the woman missionary, and are transferred as soon as possible to the local believers. Are we to stay in the shelter and comfort of our Western ivory-towers and proclaim such ministries invalid, irregular and the like? We may do so if we wish; but we shall find no warrant in the New Testament for our position. The New Testament presents to us not a hierarchy of ministers but a body of co-operating members, each exercising their God-given gifts and functions for the good of the whole and the carrying out of the work of the Servant in the world. 'It is not only the attitude of the earthly Jesus that determines this nature of all ministry in the New Testament; it is also the fact that the call to service can be understood only as an unmerited gift of grace. This is true of the calling of the disciples, according to the Synoptic testimony (Lk. 5: 8–10; Mk. 2: 14–17; Mt. 10: 8), as well as of the missions in Acts (14: 26; 15: 40; 3: 12; 14: 15), but especially in the Pauline writings. Paul knows, not only that all service is the act of God Himself (I Cor. 3: 7; 15: 9 f.), but that an essential part of the New Testament ministry is that an unqualified person is called to it 'to show that the transcendent power belongs to God and not to us' (II Cor. 4: 7).[12]

Very soon after New Testament days, however, a development set in which changed the Christian organism with its dynamic ministries into an organization with institutionalized offices. When Paul wrote to the Corinthians he urged them to submit to Christian leaders in recognition of the quality of their service (I Cor. 16: 16). When Clement wrote to the Corinthians, hardly half a century later, he urged them to reinstate their deposed presbyters because they had been properly appointed (I Clem. 44). The Christian fellowship had begun to give way to the ecclesiastical institution. The dynamic view of ministry had begun to give way to the

[11] Since the Second World War eight women to every one man have offered themselves for overseas missionary service.
[12] E. Schweizer: *op. cit.*, p. 179.

static view of 'office'. The servant had begun to savour of the master.

Two Current Dangers

If we today are to preserve the New Testament conception of a servant ministry authorized by Jesus Himself, modelled on His example, and indeed in a measure continuing His work among men,[13] we must be careful to avoid twin and opposite dangers. Both clericalism and anti-clericalism, both prelacy and anarchy, stand condemned in the light of the New Testament.

There is a tendency in some circles, and by no means only in 'Catholic' ones, for the ordained minister to lord it over the flock committed to him. Nothing can be done of any importance in the Church if he is not there. The wishes of the people in matters as widely different as ritual or policy are subordinated to his own. I know of a parish where the parochial church council does not even have its statutory say in the finances of the church; they are administered entirely by the rector. I know of another where no meeting for prayer or Bible study even in private homes is allowed by the vicar, unless he is present. These are extreme but by no means isolated examples of the danger of overvaluing the office of the ordained minister. It is, of course, bad both for the clergy and for the laity involved in such a situation. The former have an exaggerated estimate of their own importance in the Christian Body, and the latter have initiative quashed and are given little sphere in which to exercise their Christian ministry, and even less direction on how to discover it. Wherever the principle of Romans 12, of diversity in unity, is forgotten, the Church suffers. The Christian Church consists of interdependent members, and it is of the utmost importance to preserve the exercise of the different gifts the Holy Spirit has given to His people for the enrichment of the whole. When one member exceeds his place, he impoverishes the whole.

Equally dangerous, and scarcely less widespread, is a tendency to disparage the ordained ministry, which has sprung up as a reaction against clerical domination. Some Christians,

[13] So Paul, 'I will not venture to speak of anything except what Christ has wrought through me' (Rom. 15: 18). There is, in a sense, only one ministry in the Church, the ministry of Jesus carried on through the members of His Body.

notably the Brethren, have no ordained ministry at all. Others interpret the priesthood of all believers as though it meant the priesthood of no believers; while others, as B. L. Manning warned the Congregationalists, fall into the mistake of regarding the sacred ministry as a 'secretaryship, a sort of general manager's job, a device to save trouble for the majority of the church members by concentrating nearly all their duties upon one or two'.[14] This is to forget that the minister is not merely servant of the Church, but servant of Christ from whom he derives his authority, and to whom he owes supreme allegiance. In His earthly life Jesus took immense pains to train those whom He later commissioned to be apostles in His Church; after His resurrection He continued to 'give' ministers to His people (Eph. 4: 11). There are those who bear rule in the Christian churches (Heb. 13: 7; I Thes. 5: 12; I Tim. 5: 17), and consequently there are those who are ruled. The ordained ministry combines both the dignity and the lowliness of Jesus who commissions it.

Difficult though it is to reconcile these two elements in practice, it is clear that neither the complaisant nor the autocratic clergyman represents anything but a travesty of New Testament ministry. The minister must first and foremost be the servant of the Lord; and this will inevitably mean that he sets himself to be the servant of his people, dedicated to bringing them to Christian maturity and equipping them for Christian service in the world. Only in such an extension of the work of the Servant can the true balance between the authority and the lowliness of the ordained ministry be preserved.

Distortion, and often disaster, comes when the people forget that the minister is the representative of Christ to them, and when he forgets that he is called to serve.

[14] B. L. Manning: *A Layman in the Ministry*, Independent Press (1943), p. 152.

CHAPTER THREE

PRIESTS OR PRESBYTERS

A. THE THREEFOLD MINISTRY

THE Preface to the Anglican Ordinal asserts roundly, 'It is evident unto all men diligently reading the Holy Scriptures and Ancient Authors, that from the Apostles' time there have been these Orders of Ministers in Christ's Church: Bishops, Priests and Deacons.' This statement is widely misquoted as if it said, 'there have been *three* Orders'—that is, three only. The purpose of this Preface, however, is not in the least polemical. It does not set out, and the Reformers who framed it did not set out, to stigmatize, much less to unchurch, those with, for example, a presbyterian form of church government. The views of the Reformers are well known on this matter; they were agreed that all necessary doctrine was plainly set forth in Scripture, and the importance of episcopal ordination was not plainly set forth there. Thus Cranmer can say: 'I do not set more by any title, name or style than I do by the paring of an apple, further than it shall be to the setting forth of God's word and will',[1] and Bishop Hooper can write: 'I believe the Church is bound to no sort of ministers or any ordinary succession of bishops . . . but unto the only Word of God.'[2] It is significant that when the marks of the Church are given us in Article XIX there is no suggestion that any particular form of church government is essential. They are, on the contrary, precisely the same marks of the visible Church that are laid down in the Reformed Continental Confessions of Augsburg, Saxony and Switzerland. Again, Article XXIII *Of Ministering in the Congregation* reproduces a form of words from Article X (of the XLII Articles of 1553) which was deliberately designed not to exclude the Lutherans.[3]

What the Preface is concerned to maintain is that the Church of England in retaining at the Reformation the catholic orders

[1] *Remains and Letters*, p. 305.
[2] *Later Writings*, p. 90.
[3] See J. W. Hunkin: *Episcopal Ordination and Confirmation*, p. 4.

of bishop, priest and deacon, did so because they saw these orders to be agreeable both to Scripture and to history. Cranmer constantly showed his desire to abolish only what he must, and to retain, as he puts it in his Preface to the Prayer Book, what of 'the old may be well used'. Nor can his judgment be opposed on biblical or historical grounds. All three titles, though not necessarily corresponding to our conception of the offices involved, are scriptural. Moreover, not only are the names scriptural; there is a threefold division of function to be found at any rate in the later writings of the New Testament. In the Pastoral Epistles we see it most clearly. There are the presbyters or bishops; there is the subordinate ministry of deacons to assist them; and there is a superior or ordaining ministry which is exercised by Timothy and Titus (Tit. 1: 5).

If we look at the matter historically, precisely the same conclusion is reached. Nowhere do we find a 'parity of ministers'. Everywhere we find a gradation of offices in Christ's Church. The threefold ministry meets us as an established fact in the Asiatic churches at the end of the apostolic age, as the writings of Ignatius and Polycarp make plain. By the middle of the second century the threefold ministry of bishop, priest and deacon is the normal, almost universal pattern for Christian ministry the world over.

On the other hand, we must remember that other orders of ministry continue. 'Apostles', in the sense of wandering evangelists, are highly regarded in the *Didache* (11:3). There are still prophets and prophetesses,[4] still exorcists and miraculous healers towards the end of the second century. Witnesses as far apart as Justin in Rome,[5] Irenaeus in Gaul,[6] and Tertullian in North Africa[7] not only attest the fact but regard them as part of Christ's gift to His Church. Irenaeus is quite prepared to recognize some of his contemporaries as possessing the 'divinely bestowed power of prophesying'; in this case they 'speak when and where God pleases'.[8] Ignatius is aware that, when preaching to the Philadelphians the spirit of prophecy came upon him, and he cried out 'with the voice of God.'[9]

[4] See A. Ehrhardt: *The Apostolic Succession*, chapter 4.
[5] *Dial.* 38, 82.
[6] *Adv. Haer.* 2.32.4, 5.
[7] *De Anima* 9.
[8] *Adv. Haer.* 1.13.4.
[9] *Philad.* 7.

The four prophesying daughters of Philip (Acts 21: 9) made a great impression on the second-century Church, a Church which could not deny the possibility of a resurgence of prophecy in the Montanist movement, and therefore concentrated on launching personal attacks on the principal Montanists! It is interesting, furthermore, as a corrective to the common view which sees the prophetic and settled ministries as essentially incompatible with one another, to remember that the Montanists combined their emphasis on the prophetic office with a retention of the threefold orders of the catholic Church; the two remain side by side, of course, in the *Didache* as well.

Furthermore, even the Roman Catholic Church does not recognize only three orders, but rather divides ministries into major and minor. The major orders include a fourth office, that of sub-deacon, in addition to those of bishop, priest and deacon.[10] Indeed, many eminent Catholic theologians, including Thomas Aquinas, have refused to regard the episcopate as a separate order distinct from the priesthood. Jerome took this position with truly Presbyterian fervour, and the Council of Trent defined that bishops and presbyters differ in *gradus* but not in *ordo*.[11] It would be precarious, therefore, to interpret the Anglican Ordinal in any exclusive sense. This can easily be proved, if proof be needed, by the fact that the Church of England in the sixteenth and seventeenth centuries enjoyed the closest of relationships, including intercommunion and occasional exchange of ministers (without reordination), with Reformed churches on the Continent who had not retained the threefold ministry. What we may maintain with confidence, however, is that the threefold ministry is securely grounded both in Scripture and history; and so, without prejudice to other ministries, we shall proceed to examine those of bishop, priest and deacon.

B. THE PRIEST OR PRESBYTER

We shall take first the priest or presbyter, for he is the minister who meets us most frequently in the pages of the New Testament. As we shall see later, the Christian priest has nothing

---

[10] In the Roman Church of the mid-third century we find a fascinating catalogue of ministries: 46 presbyters, 7 deacons, 7 sub-deacons, 42 acolytes, and 52 exorcists, readers and doorkeepers (Eusebius, *H.E.* 6: 43).

[11] *Session* 23, esp. chapter 2.

to do with the sacrificing priesthood of the Old Testament. The word is derived both historically and linguistically from the 'presbyter' or 'elder' of the New Testament.

1. Presbyters in Judaism

There is general agreement that the Church took over this office of presbyter from the organization of the Jewish synagogue. In the early days, Christians must have been regarded as simply another of the many groups within Judaism, distinguished by their peculiar belief that Jesus was the long awaited Messiah. Any ten Jewish men could band together to form a synagogue—we find a varied list of some of the Jerusalem synagogues in Acts 6: 9—so it is hardly surprising that in Jewish areas Christian congregations were long called synagogues (Jas. 2: 2). Now the civil and administrative duties of the synagogue devolved upon a board of presbyters. They saw that the Law was observed, administered taxes, represented the synagogue in relations with pagan authorities, and in their hands lay the right of excommunication. It is not clear, however, that they had any liturgical function. The responsibility for public worship and the task of presiding at it fell to a quite different official, the 'ruler of the synagogue' (cf. Lk. 8: 41). He was not a priest of the Aaronic line; he was another layman who was elected for the office.

2. Presbyters in the Early Church

It seems clear, then, that the Jewish presbyterate was the model taken over by the early Christians and adapted for their own purposes. This probably happened first in Jerusalem, as Luke suggests (in Acts 11: 30 the presbyters of the Jerusalem church are mentioned without any introduction or explanation). The system proved satisfactory, and was widely used in Christian congregations as they spread throughout the Mediterranean basin. We find presbyters in Ephesus (Acts 20: 17), presbyters throughout Asia Minor (I Pet. 5: 1 cf. 1: 1), presbyters among the Jewish Dispersion (Jas. 5: 14 cf. 1: 1). We find Paul and Barnabas 'appointing elders in every church' on the First Missionary Journey (Acts 14: 23). So universal is the pattern that we find them figuring prominently in John's vision of heaven, where the four and twenty elders (the representative numbers of the Old and New Covenants) worship God continually (Rev. 4: 4, etc.).

If this is so, why do we find no mention of presbyters in Paul's letters (apart from the Pastoral Epistles)? A number of considerations may help to answer this at first rather surprising fact. Chance may have something to do with it. We would have no mention of 'bishops' either, if Philippians had not been preserved. But, more important, it seems probable that the presbyters (or elders) were called bishops (or overseers) in Gentile churches, for that word was commonly used to denote any sort of supervision in the Graeco-Roman world. It is certainly interesting that at Philippi (Phil. 1: 1), in Asia Minor (Acts 20: 28; I Pet. 2: 25, 5: 2), and in Crete (Tit. 1: 7) the presbyter is called bishop. As we shall see later, the two offices were the same, and it was merely a difference of nomenclature in Jewish and Gentile churches. However, 'bishop' never completely replaced 'presbyter' even among Gentile congregations (I Tim. 5: 17; I Clem. 21: 44).

Furthermore, there is a variety of expression in the New Testament, and particularly among the Pauline circle, to denote the ministerial office. The function is so much more important than the name. We are probably right in seeing the presbyter in the 'leader' of Hebrews 13: 7, 17, the 'man who bears rule' of I Thessalonians 5: 12, 13, and Romans 12: 8, while the 'pastors and teachers' of Ephesians 4: 11 is almost certainly a hendiadys for the same office.[12] Again, we should probably regard the 'helps and leaderships' of I Corinthians 12: 28 as two sorts of divine gifts which soon crystallized in the diaconate and presbyterate respectively.

Of these names the most interesting is 'those who bear rule'. The *proistamenos* (and its cognate form *prostates*) originally denoted the powerful Roman 'patron' who had his 'clients', and the word then came to be used widely of any person of wealth and influence, who exerted himself on behalf of poorer, weaker friends. Once Clement applies it to Jesus, whom he calls 'the patron of our weakness' (36: 1). The word sheds a fine light on the nature of Christian leadership. It is no doubt because of her championing the cause of her poorer and less influential Christian friends that Phoebe, the deaconess of the church at Cenchreae, is given this lovely title (Rom. 16: 2).

[12] Thus the task of acting as 'pastor' is assigned to presbyter/bishops in Acts 20: 28, I Pet. 5: 2, while teaching is always regarded as a prime function of a presbyter/bishop (I Tim. 3: 2; 5: 17).

37

3. *The Task of the Presbyters*

These different titles give us some idea of the job of the minister. He is, first and foremost, a *presbyter*, and the word meant primarily a senior, an elderly man. Indeed, it is notoriously difficult to know whether age or office is meant in some of the New Testament references to presbyters. Thus in I Timothy 5: 1–3 it is clearly an older man that is in view, but v. 17 of the same chapter equally clearly points to a specific office. The same ambiguity is present in I Peter 5: 1–5, and this suggests that the elders were normally drawn from among the senior men in the congregation. One was considered a young man in both Greek and Hebrew culture until past the age of forty.

Then the title *bishop* describes the main function of these elders (Acts 20: 28; I Pet. 5: 2, see p. 42 f.). They are to superintend and oversee the Christian congregations committed to them. It has often been remarked that presbyter more properly describes the *office*, and bishop the *function* of the early Christian minister. This oversight will mean that they are *pastors* (I Pet. 5: 2; Acts 20: 28) who feed the flock with the Word of God, and *leaders* in every Christian enterprise, not least, no doubt, in public worship. They are to act like *patron* to client, and this will involve both material assistance when needed, and the ministry of admonition to the unruly (I Thess. 5: 12) and support for the weak (Acts 20: 35). Theirs is supremely a teaching office (I Tim. 3: 2; Tit. 1: 9), and this grows more important as the Church spreads and the apostles die out. Thus their work is in some ways parallel to, and in some ways much wider than that of the Jewish elder. Both bear rule, both have administrative functions, both excommunicate (this is hinted at, perhaps, in I Cor. 5: 4, 5); both, no doubt, have the task of representing their communities to pagans. But unlike the Jewish presbyters the Christian minister has a pastoral and probably a liturgical function as well. Unlike them he is supremely a teacher; unlike them he is entrusted with a specific ministry of prayer (Jas. 5: 14). Perhaps the greatest difference was this: all Christian rule was marked with the imprint of Jesus the Servant. Had He not both told them and demonstrated to them (Lk. 22: 26) that the leader (*hegoumenos*) among them was to adopt the role of the servant (*diakonos*)? How could they ever forget, when they used this

38

title *hegoumenos* of Christian presbyters, that its supremacy was one of service? How could they ever be domineering over the flock in their work as bishops (I Pet. 5: 3) whilst they kept in mind the type of oversight exercised by Jesus, the Bishop of their souls (I Pet. 2: 25)?

4. *Presbyters — a Corporate and Settled Ministry*

Two further points emerge clearly from the New Testament evidence we are considering. The first is that the presbyters are the settled ministry of the Church, as opposed to the itinerant apostles, evangelists and prophets. This holds good of every place where they are mentioned in the New Testament. It is particularly noticeable in the Jerusalem church, where, in the absence of the apostles on missionary journeys we read simply of the presbyters (Acts 11: 30) or James and the presbyters (Acts 21: 17).

The second point, too, is noteworthy; these Christian ministers always appear in the plural. The Jewish presbyteral system is maintained by the Church throughout all the variety of nomenclature. There are two apparent exceptions, which prove to have no substance upon examination. In I Timothy 3: 2 and in Titus 1: 7 the 'bishop' appears in the singular, and from this some have assumed that here we have an officer different from (and superior to) the presbyters. It is clear, however, when the context is examined, that this is not the case. For in Titus 1: 5–7 Titus is ordered to ordain 'presbyters in every city . . . if any be blameless . . . for a bishop must be blameless . . .' In other words, the singular is a generalizing singular, and the presbyters and the bishop are one and the same here as they are in the rest of the New Testament. The other rather strange use of elder in the singular comes in II John 1 and III John 1. The author is apparently so well known that he can simply call himself *the* Elder without fear of being misunderstood. How can this be? Archbishop Carrington has shewn, in the last chapter of his *Primitive Christian Catechism*, that the Church took over the Jewish system of teaching or *tannaite* elders. A famous rabbi like Hillel is often called in an absolute sense '*the* elder'. It seems likely that the John who wrote these letters acquired in Asia a teaching authority equal to that of Hillel among the Jews, and was simply known as *The Elder*. Indeed, this honorific title did not soon die out. Irenaeus calls the bishops of Rome by it, and Hippolytus' favourite name for his master Irenaeus is 'the elder'. It is the affectionate title of respect accorded to the most influential teacher of his age and is used irrespective of whether the recipient be apostle, bishop or presbyter.

5. Two Types of Presbyter?

One question remains. Does the New Testament teach that there were originally two types of elder, corresponding to the lay or ruling elders and the ministerial or teaching elders of Calvin (*Institutes*, Book IV), and some of the Presbyterian churches? The question largely turns on the interpretation of I Timothy 5: 17, 'Let the elders who rule well be considered worthy of double honour [or *pay*], especially those who labour in preaching and teaching.' There can be little doubt that it is the function of all elders to 'rule'. It seems, however, to be strongly implied that not all elders 'labour' (a technical term for ministerial activity—I Thess. 5: 12; Gal. 4: 11, etc.) at preaching and teaching. Does this mean that there is an *élite* within the presbyteral board which *does* spend itself in preaching and teaching? Lightfoot regards this view as untenable,[13] and there is certainly little enough in the rest of the New Testament to support it; many modern Presbyterian writers are also included to abandon it.[14] Nevertheless, it cannot be denied that Cyprian knows of *presbyteri doctores*, teaching elders, as opposed to other presbyters,[15] and this may well have come down from early times. Certainly it makes clear that even in his day there were some presbyters who did not belong to the class of teachers. This becomes all the more plausible when we recall the distinction between tannaite and non-tannaite elders within Judiasm which Carrington argues was carried into Christianity. Whether, therefore, we believe there were two classes of elders in the early Church, or whether, with Lightfoot, we interpret this verse as meaning 'as each had his special gift, so would he devote himself more or less exclusively to the one or the other of these sacred functions', does not make a great deal of difference in the last analysis. On any showing the presbyterate of the early Church exercised a far more corporate oversight than that of most Anglican

[13] *Op. cit.*, pp. 22 f.
[14] See *A Manual of Church Doctrine according to the Church of Scotland*, ed. Torrance and Wright (1960), p. 100.
[15] *Ep.* 29.

incumbents and their church councils. The virtual autocracy of many a parish priest today is good neither for him nor for the parish; it is clearly at variance with the pattern of the priesthood in the New Testament; and it obscures the fact that he is called to serve.

CHAPTER FOUR

BISHOPS

1. *Presbyter-Bishops in the New Testament*

In the New Testament bishops and presbyters are the same. This, as Lightfoot has shewn, is the plain meaning of Scripture. His conclusions are accepted even by representative Roman Catholic authorities like the *Catholic Dictionary*, and the attempt of Dr. Austin Farrer in *The Apostolic Ministry* to overthrow it can only be described as an ingenious *tour de force* which has failed to convince anybody. Even he admits (p. 168) that he has not proved his case!

The evidence upon which the identification of presbyter and bishop is based is as follows. In Acts 20 the elders of v. 17 (*presbyteroi*) are called to exercise the function of bishops in v. 28 (*episkopountes*). In I Peter 5: 1, 2 the presbyters are again, in most manuscripts, told to act as bishops of the flock, though some important manuscripts omit the word *episkopountes*.[1] In I Timothy 3: 1–7 we have a description of a bishop, followed immediately by the requirements for a deacon, while in 5: 17–19 the former ministers are referred to and given the name of presbyters. Titus, as we have seen, is told to 'appoint elders in every town . . . for a bishop must be blameless' (Tit. 1: 5–7). It is interesting that Jerome in his commentary on this passage, says plainly, '*Idem est ergo presbyter qui episcopus*'—'the bishop, therefore, is the same as the presbyter', and his view was widely shared in the Church. The identity of presbyters and bishops is the obvious conclusion to be drawn from Philippians 1: 1: 'to all the saints in Christ Jesus who are at Philippi, with the bishops and deacons'. We can hardly imagine the apostle singling out the first and third orders of the ministry with a plurality of bishops thrown in as an extra anomaly! Clement of Rome at the end of the first century knows no difference between the orders. Three times

---

[1] If the word is not part of the original text, its later inclusion is all the more impressive, because so soon the office of bishop became separate from that of presbyter.

he mentions bishops and deacons together as in Philippians, which is all the more striking because the whole object of his letter is to secure the reinstatement of the deposed presbyters (chapters 42–44). In the *Didache*, too, we meet just two orders, bishops and deacons. As late as the fourth century some memories of this early use survive. The *Apostolic Constitutions* (2: 26, 28) state that it is the presbyters who stand in the place of the apostles. This is not an anti-episcopal claim, but rather a recognition that presbyters and bishops were, in New Testament times, a single order.

2. *Monepiscopacy from the Second Century*

Nevertheless, it must be recognized that by the very beginning of the second century a new phraseology begins. The letters of Ignatius, whose lifetime certainly overlapped considerably with that of St. John, make it certain that monepiscopacy, rule by a single bishop, was a regular feature in the churches of Asia Minor in his own day. As bishop he writes to the bishops of Ephesus, Philadelphia, and so forth. He is almost obsessed with the importance of the episcopate, and he often speaks with great clarity about the threefold ministry. Thus in *Magn.* 6 he urges his readers to 'do all things in unity, under the bishop presiding in the place of God, the presbyters in the place of the Council of the Apostles, and the deacons . . . who are entrusted with the service (*diakonia*) of Jesus Christ'. Though he himself has nothing to say about apostolic succession, we learn from Tertullian (*Adv. Marc.* 4: 5) and Clement of Alexandria (in Eusebius *H.E.* 3: 23) that the Apostle John went round in his old age appointing bishops in Asia Minor. If this were not the case, it seems almost incredible that they should have become so marked a feature of Roman Asia within such a few years of the death of the apostle, although Streeter is probably right in suspecting that the very stress laid by Ignatius upon the indispensability of the bishop is an indication that monepiscopacy is not yet really as firmly established as he would wish (*The Primitive Church*, p. 173 ff.). Indeed, early as its appearance is in the East, it may well have come to the West considerably later. The Roman church was governed by a board of presbyters in the closing years of the first century, as we have seen in I Clement. The same holds good thirty or forty years later when Hermas wrote. He twice refers to bishops, each time in the plural (*Vis.* 3.5.1; *Sim.*

43

9.27.2), and otherwise refers either to the 'elders who preside over the Church' (*Vis.* 2.4) or to 'the rulers of the Church that occupy the chief seats' (*Vis.* 3.9.7). Dr. Telfer, after a careful examination of the evidence, concludes that monarchical episcopacy came to the West almost a generation after Ignatius, and owed a good deal to his teaching on episcopacy which he sealed with his martyrdom (*The Office of a Bishop*, p. 88 ff.). It is interesting that whereas Ignatius could write to the bishop in the Eastern churches, he could not do so—and does not do so—in his letter to the Romans. The same holds good of his contemporary Polycarp. Though himself a bishop in the Ignatian sense (Ignatius, *Polyc.* 1: 1), he knows that this form of polity does not pertain at Philippi. And so, with gracious Christian tact, he begins his letter: 'Polycarp and the presbyters with him, to the Church of God sojourning at Philippi'; he makes no mention of the bishop anywhere in his letter, but refers to the Philippians' own ministers as presbyters (6: 1) and deacons (5: 2). That was in A.D. 115. It is plain that monepiscopacy was unevenly distributed in the first half of the second century.

3. *The Background of Monepiscopacy*

What is the background of this office that springs immediately to full flower in the pages of Ignatius? The problem is notoriously difficult. There is no obvious parallel in Judaism. Attempts have certainly been made to seek a model in the ruler of the Jewish synagogue who presided over worship and acted as arbiter in synagogue affairs; furthermore, he had an assistant, the *hazzan* who would, on this showing, prove an admirable prototype for the deacon. However, the work of the Christian bishop could no more be derived from that of the ruler of the synagogue than the title *episkopos* from that of *archisynagogos*. A more hopeful source is suggested by the 'overseer' of the Qumran community, particularly since there is increasing evidence of connections between the men of Qumran and the early Christians. At the head of each group of Covenanters, as they were called, was a *mebhakkēr* (overseer or bishop) who presided at meetings and was probably concerned with admission of new members.[2] The Church may possibly have derived the title from this source, but the corporate nature of

[2] See H. H. Rowley: *From Moses to Qumran*, Lutterworth (1963), p. 256.

the New Testament episcopate shows that this solution is no more probable than the last. Monepiscopacy owes more to the precedent set by James of Jerusalem.

4. The Position of James, the Lord's Brother

Eusebius,[3] Epiphanius,[4] Chrysostom[5] and Jerome[6] all agree in seeing James as the first bishop of Jerusalem; their accounts differ as to whether he was instituted by the apostles or by the Lord Himself. The evidence is complex, and recent treatments of it have produced radically different results, as may be seen by consulting Telfer's *The Office of a Bishop*, Ehrhardt's *The Apostolic Succession*, Cullmann's *Peter* and Karrer's *Peter and the Church*. What does seem to be clear is this: We know from John 7: 5 that James, along with the other brothers of the Lord, did not believe in Him during His ministry. We know from I Corinthians 15: 7 that the risen Christ appeared to him. From then on he meets us as a Christian. Indeed, in a remarkably short time he rose to a position of extraordinary eminence in the Church. Paul mentions him before Peter and John when he speaks of the 'pillars' of the Jerusalem Church (Gal. 2: 9). Luke (Acts 15: 13–21) records his presidency at the Apostolic Council of apostles and elders at Jerusalem in the late 40's. He is in undisputed leadership of the Jerusalem Church, in fact, after the departure of Peter from Jerusalem (Acts 12: 17). Acts 21: 18 ff. make this particularly obvious. He had, we learn from our scanty extra-biblical sources, a remarkable reputation for piety among non-Christian Jewry; he was so distinguished that he could write a general letter headed 'James, a servant of God and of the Lord Jesus Christ', and everyone would know who was meant; and he left an unparalleled impression on Jewish Christians as the Pseudo-Clementines make plain; to them he is the 'bishop of bishops'.

When we ask what was the reason for this remarkable ascendancy, we shall not find the answer in his undoubted holiness, nor yet in his possible membership of the apostolic band (the meaning of Gal. 1: 19 is ambiguous). He was the nearest male relation to the Saviour. Herein lay his great influence, particularly in a society as dedicated to family

[3] *H.E.* 7: 19.
[4] *Panarion* 78: 7.
[5] *Hom.* 38: 4.
[6] *De Vir. Ill.* 2.

solidarity as were the Jews. It is not without significance that Paul calls him 'the Lord's brother'. If confirmation were wanted that his physical relationship to Jesus was of supreme importance, it is provided by the fact that after his martyrdom 'Symeon, the son of Cleophas, our Lord's uncle, was appointed the second bishop, whom all proposed, as the cousin of the Lord'.[7] Clearly the Jewish Church adopted what Streeter has aptly called a 'caliphate', and if we take the hints given in other parts of the New Testament (for example Mk. 3: 31 ff.; II Cor. 5: 16; Gal. 2: 5–9), we may believe that this was strongly resented in some parts, at least, of the Gentile church. To the claim of the Pseudo-Clementines that James is the bishop of bishops, the Gentile reaction is reflected in the question discussed by Origen, whether a Jewish believer could possibly be a Christian at all. Origen thought he could, but was aware that he was presenting a minority report![8] Jerome is, characteristically, less charitable.[9] While, therefore, there is little doubt that James furnished an obvious precedent for second-century bishops, with his settled abode at Jerusalem, his wide supervision, and his constitutional rule together with the elders (Acts 21: 18), nevertheless, in fact, by his physical connection with the Lord, and because of the destruction of his line in the early years of the second century, he represented the very antithesis of the emerging monepiscopacy of the Catholic Church.

5. The Growth of Monepiscopacy

If the precedents for this office are obscure, so are the stages by which it became separated from the presbyterate. How did *episkope*, the oversight originally vested in all the presbyters, become concentrated in the hands of one? The question has been endlessly debated; the almost complete lack of evidence leaves us very much in the dark, and we can at best deal with probabilities. Certain things, however, are self-evident. If you have a board of elders, one man must obviously preside; otherwise nothing gets done. It is therefore, as Lightfoot saw, most probable that the monarchical bishop arose out of the board of presbyters by virtue of his chairmanship. When we

[7] Eusebius: *H.E.* 4: 22.
[8] See his *Contra Celsum* 2: 1; 5: 61, 65.
[9] *Ep. ad August.* 89. 'They want to be both Christians and Jews. In fact they are neither.'

come to the second century, we find that the bishop is constantly associated with certain activities which would tend to emphasize his supremacy. First and foremost, the bishop is always the president at the eucharist which, from the nature of the case, requires a single celebrant. Secondly, the bishop is always in charge of the property of the church. This remained very little until the very end of the second century, when permanent buildings for worship began to be built. It consisted in the early days almost entirely of the gifts of the Christians in money and kind at the holy communion, and these, naturally, were administered by the bishop as the celebrant. Thirdly, we find the bishop acting as the focus of unity amid the varying sectional interests and, in the early days, house churches of a large town. 'Do nothing without the bishop,' cries Ignatius; 'cherish union; shun divisions' (*Philad.* 7). Fourthly, he appears as the bastion of orthodoxy, the guardian of the apostolic message, particularly in the centuries before an authoritative canon of Scripture was universally recognized. The succession of bishops in a see was regarded, particularly by Irenaeus, as a safeguard against the heretical intrusions of the Gnostics, and a guarantee of continuity with the teachings of the apostolic age. Fifthly, the bishop always appears as, so to speak, the foreign secretary of his church;[10] through him it communicates with others, and through him visitors from other churches are welcomed, and hospitality found for them. In some such ways as these, we may believe, the chairman of the presbyters became the bishop of Catholic Christendom.

6. *The Theory of Monepiscopacy*

But what was the theory behind it? I believe that, quite simply, the idea of sole episcopacy originated in the sole oversight of God Himself. In the New Testament, *episkope* and its cognates are more than once referred to the Holy Trinity. Almighty God oversees the world, and will judge it (Lk. 19: 44; I Pet. 2: 12). Jesus Christ exercises a shepherd's loving oversight over His people (I Pet. 2: 25), while the Holy Spirit sets apart men to exercise this oversight in the Church (Acts 20: 28) as the undershepherds of Christ (I Pet. 5: 4). *Episkope*, therefore, is an attribute of God Himself which in

[10] So Hermas *Vis.* 2: 4: 'Clement will send his [copy] to the foreign countries, for commission has been given to him to do so . . .'

His grace He delegates to some members of His Church. Indeed, it may well be argued that *episkope* belongs to *all* Christians;[11] such seems to be the plain inference from the use of the verb in Matthew 25: 36, 43, James 1: 27 and Hebrews 12: 15. Moulton and Milligan quote papyrus examples of the use of the verb as a common closing salutation meaning to 'look after so and so'. This seems to be the force of Hebrews 12: 15, 'See to it that there is none of your number who . . .' It would seem that, like servanthood and priesthood, oversight belongs to the whole Church. If this is the case, then the supreme oversight is indeed God's, Father, Son and Holy Spirit. He delegates it to the Church, without surrendering His responsibility, and the Church delegates it to the ministry, again without surrendering its own responsibility. No wonder, then, that Paul wrote: 'If anyone aspires to *episkope*, he desires a noble task' (I Tim. 3: 1). No wonder Ignatius exclaims that the bishop is the type, the representative, of God the Father (*Magn.* 6: 1; *Trall.* 3: 1).[12]

7. *The Value of Monepiscopacy*

Therefore, although the Ignatian type of episcopacy can neither be found in the New Testament nor in many parts of the early Church for a long time to come, nevertheless it remains true that the New Testament does know of pastoral oversight exercised by the apostles and their delegates over local ministers. The need for this sort of oversight increased with the death of the last apostles. With the spread of the Church throughout the world there is more than ever a need for a focus of unity within the churches of a given area. There is still the need to defend the apostolic faith against attenuation or perversion, though whether the episcopate has been particularly successful in this respect down the centuries, and particularly at the present day, may be doubted.[13] Most important of all is the crying need for a ministry to ministers, an oversight of overseers, as none know better than the clergy.

[11] I owe this suggestion to the Rev. J. R. W. Stott.

[12] Ignatius is expressing this same conviction in another way when he says that after his martyrdom the church in Syria will have God for its Shepherd and Christ for its Bishop *in his place*! (Rom. 9: 1).

[13] As the Minority Report in the Anglican-Methodist Conversations puts it (*Report*, p. 58), historic episcopacy 'has notoriously failed to act as the safeguard it is claimed to be. This is sufficiently illustrated by the history of the medieval and renaissance papacy'.

On these grounds it can be urged that not merely the name but the office of bishop is scriptural, primitive, and of abiding value in the Church.

This is becoming increasingly recognized among Free Churchmen. There *is* value in monepiscopacy, and clearly it is the only form of church government that can possibly command universal consent in the reunion of Christendom. But that is not to say that episcopacy as we know it in England is commendable. The larger the diocese, the less justification there is for monepiscopacy. Sole leadership of a million or more people cannot possibly be pastoral, and runs great danger of becoming prelatical. This has been a weakness in English episcopacy for years. Very often counsel is darkened because the Ignatian arguments are applied to the present scheme of things in England, and it is forgotten that episcopacy to Ignatius is more like a vicar's presidency over half a dozen curates than diocesan episcopacy where the bishop presides (if the word is meaningful in such a context) over hundreds of local churches. Ignatius does not speak to our condition, for he does not speak of our sort of bishops. The collegiate nature of Ignatian episcopacy is in sore need of being recovered in England. Twelve times in his epistles does he mention the three orders of ministry, and in ten of them they form an inseparable unity — the other two references are indecisive. We could not realize this today without far smaller bishoprics — the size, perhaps, of an archdeaconry, coupled with some form of synodical government.

The present drift (particularly evident in current ecclesiastical legislation) away from this collegiate conception of oversight in the Church, and the tendency to remove power from the hands of the parish clergy and concentrate it in the hands of the episcopate (with all the growth of ecclesiastical bureaucracy that inevitably accompanies it) is most unhealthy. The Free Churchman regards it with suspicion, and feels that the growing transformation of the bishop from the 'undershepherd' into the 'lord' of the flock is derogatory to the supreme headship of Christ over His Church. The Eastern Orthodox would be equally dissatisfied with our system. For although they retain a hierarchy of ministries, they recognize that it is the Church as a whole, and not the clergy, let alone the episcopate, who are the inheritors of the truth of God. The bishop is nothing without the laity, nor the laity without the bishop, through whom they are linked to the world-wide Church. The bishops in ecumenical council may seek to define more clearly some aspect of the truth of God, but these definitions must then be acclaimed and lived by the whole people of God before they are recognized as the voice of the Church. This solidarity between bishop and people has nothing quite like it in the West, and their Consecration Prayer that the new bishop may, like the Good Shepherd, lay down his life for the sheep, instruct them faithfully, and in the Day of Judgment be able to hold up his head among those 'who have suffered for the preaching of Thy Gospel' shows that the Eastern Church has come very near the New Testament pattern of the bishop as a leader who is called to serve his people; a pastor who knows, loves, teaches and suffers with his flock.

CHAPTER FIVE

DEACONS

OUR knowledge of the deacon in the primitive Church is as scanty as it is of the bishop, but for a different reason. As we have seen, service (*diakonia*) was the ideal and the task of every member of the Church, and there was no immediate tendency to restrict the title to any particular group within it.

The word 'deacon' is used of Jesus Himself (Rom. 15: 8; Gal. 2: 17), and in consequence is applied very naturally in the New Testament to any kind of service done for His sake. To be sure, in Philippians 1: 1 it does appear to denote a special order of ministry, and in I Timothy 3: 8–13 this is even more obvious. Nevertheless, as if to warn us that the word is still used only in a semi-technical sense, we find Timothy, only a few verses later, being called a deacon (I Tim. 4: 6), while in 1: 12 Paul has used the word to describe his own ministry! Nothing could demonstrate more clearly that the pattern of the Servant was normative for *all* Christian ministry.

1. *An Auxiliary Ministry*

Nevertheless, despite these ambiguities, it is plain from the New Testament that there are ministries of leadership and ministries of assistance, superior and subordinate functions within the Body. The differentiation is first emphasized in Acts 6: 1 ff., where the apostles find the administration of the infant Church too time-consuming and seek out men full of the Spirit to whom they can delegate the financial and administrative tasks arising from the communism of goods practised for a while by the Jerusalem church. Leaving aside the question whether these Seven are to be regarded as deacons in the technical sense, we have here a prime example of the institution of a subordinate and auxiliary ministry, for the Seven are set aside to '*deacon*' tables, thus releasing the apostles for the task of '*deaconing*' the Word (Acts 6: 4).

We find the same differentiation in I Corinthians 12: 28.

Some are given by the Lord the task of being 'rulers' among His people, others are 'helps'. It is possible that in Romans 12: 7 the diaconate is contrasted with the ministry of teaching and exhortation, and the vagueness of St. Paul's language may be due to the fact that he was unaware of the titles given in the Roman church to those who performed these two functions. In Philippians 1: 1, written at much the same time, Paul knows whom he is addressing; they are bishops and deacons. But the same distinction between those who lead and those who assist is present. So, too, in I Timothy 3, we find the diaconate ranged alongside the episcopate as an auxiliary office, though, rather curiously, in the letter to Titus it is not mentioned.

2. *Its Origin*

Some liturgiologists have sought the origin of the deacon in the *ḥazzan* or attendant of the synagogue. This would be suitable enough precedent as far as the liturgical functions of the deacon are concerned, were it not for the fact that where the synagogue attendant is actually mentioned in the New Testament, *ḥazzan* is translated not by *diakonos*, but by a quite different word, *huperetes* (Lk. 4: 20)! In any case it would provide no precedent at all for the administrative and pastoral duties of the Christian deacon. It seems evident that precise analogies are not to be sought outside Christianity; otherwise it would be hard to explain why Clement of Rome (chapter 42) finds it necessary to introduce deacons by force into the text of Isaiah 60: 17!

It is difficult to decide whether Luke thinks of the Seven of Acts 6 as the first Christian deacons. It would be very helpful if so; for it would tell us that deacons were ordained by prayer and the imposition of hands; that they had to be wise men full of the Holy Spirit; and that their functions besides being financial and administrative, involved preaching and disputing with the Jews, evangelism and the performance of wonders and miracles (Acts 6: 7–10; 21: 8). The later Church from Irenaeus onwards certainly saw these Seven as deacons, so much so that there was a tendency in more than one great church of the Roman empire to restrict the number of deacons to seven.[1] Furthermore, there is substance in Lightfoot's contention that

[1] The Council of Neo-Caesarea in A.D. 315 passed as one of its canons: 'The deacons ought to be seven, even if the city be great.'

the prominent position given by Luke to this incident is designed to draw attention to the creation of a new office, while the incidental mention of the presbyters in Acts 11: 30 is casual and allusive simply because they do *not* represent a new departure, but are modelled on the presbyters so familiar to Judaism.

Nevertheless, it is a plain fact that the Seven are not called deacons in Acts 6; their functions of preaching and evangelism hardly correspond with the duties assigned to the later diaconate; and when Philip, 'one of the Seven', is mentioned later in the narrative, he is described not as 'the deacon' but as 'the evangelist' (21: 8). No confident conclusion can be drawn on this point, but if the appointment of the Seven is dissociated from the institution of the diaconate, we have no knowledge whatever of the origin of the office, and can only assume from Philippians 1: 1 that this was the name given to a subsidiary office which assisted the presbyter-bishops particularly in financial matters.[2]

3. *Its Function*

The Seven were appointed in the first instance to supervise and administer poor relief. Men like Stephen and Philip would turn to good account the opportunities that came their way as they moved in and out among the poor believers, and so, as Lightfoot has it, 'without ceasing to be dispensers of alms, they became also ministers of the Word'. Whether or not the Seven were deacons, this task of a subsidiary ministry engaged primarily on poor relief fits in well with such scanty references to their function as we find elsewhere in the New Testament. As we have seen, it accords well enough with Philippians 1: 1, and is no less appropriate in I Timothy 3: 8–13. Here it is required that a deacon should be consistent in what he says, and not greedy for money, both important qualities in a man who was constantly moving from house to house and distributing financial help. We are not told that he must be talented at preaching or teaching, but we are told that his life must be exemplary, and that his grasp of the Christian faith must be sound and comprehensive. Because of the pastoral nature of

[2] Paul's letter to the Philippians is a thank-you letter for a contribution given him by the church; and it is reasonable to see the 'bishops and deacons' as the organizers of that collection; hence their separate mention in 1: 1.

their work it is important that deacons be sober, balanced men, aware of the dangers of drink and gossip, cherishing a pure conscience before God, and of unimpeachable character before men. That is why they must be subjected to careful scrutiny before they are accepted for the office.

In subsequent generations we find the deacons closely associated with the bishop whose assistants they are in both administrative and liturgical functions. Indeed, this close association with the bishop led not infrequently to a deacon succeeding to the bishopric without ever being ordained priest. Two things are never forgotten about them; they represent the ministry of the Servant Jesus in His Church,[3] and their supposed origin in 'serving tables' is remembered both in the part they play in administering the holy communion, and in the task which Justin[4] tells us fell to them afterwards, of taking the consecrated elements to any who were unable through sickness to be present at communion.

In the early Church a man would often remain a deacon for life, and so it remains in the Eastern church, where the deacon does a 'lay' job. However, in Western Christendom the office merely became a stepping stone to the priesthood, as, indeed, it still remains in the Roman and Anglican churches.[5] At the Reformation some attempt was made to recover the primitive diaconate, and in Congregational and Baptist churches today the word 'deacon' is used to denote what the Presbyterian churches prefer to call 'elder'. This is a 'lay' office, and does not normally lead into the ordained ministry. Such a man is a representative of the congregation who takes part with the ordained ministry in three ways in particular: by assisting in exercising discipline, by undertaking administrative work, and by distributing the elements at holy communion. The diaconate of the New Testament is awaiting rediscovery within our Church, and should become subject for serious

[3] Ignatius is at pains to emphasize the parallel between the deacons and Jesus. They are 'entrusted with the *diakonia* of Jesus Christ' (*Magn.* 6: 1).

[4] *I Apology*, 65.

[5] One widely accepted explanation of I Timothy 3: 13 would suggest that Paul saw the diaconate as a stepping stone to full oversight. This appears to be an anachronism, and the verse probably means that those who have served well as deacons will gain a good standing for themselves; they will find it, like oversight (3: 1), a thoroughly rewarding task.

study and research in a communion that professes such respect for the threefold historic ministry.

4. *Deaconesses*

There is evidence to suggest that the primitive diaconate included women. In Romans 16: 1 Paul speaks of Phoebe as a woman who clearly held some official position, and was about to be sent by him on definite Church work (traditionally to deliver his letter to the Romans). He describes her as *diakonos* of the church at Cenchreae, and most commentators agree in seeing this as the title of her office. Furthermore, the context of I Timothy 3: 11 and the way in which it is phrased makes it likely that Paul is speaking not of the wives of deacons (to whom he alludes in v. 12), but to woman deacons. Certainly the Greek fathers took this verse to refer to deaconesses; the absence of the definite article would make the translation 'their wives' very harsh, and no one has explained why, if the wives of deacons are meant here, the apostle omits to mention the wives of bishops who would, presumably, have an even more important role. No, we must see this as a reference to deaconesses, and we know from Pliny's letter (10: 96), written about A.D. 112, that there was such an order of ministry in the early Church. He tells us that he examined under torture two deaconesses (*ministrae*). Their value was, of course, immense in an oriental culture which kept women in considerable seclusion. In later times they visited, instructed and assisted at the baptism of woman adherents to the faith. Doubtless, they did the same in the early days as well.

The pattern for such ministry of women is afforded by Luke 8:3. It was not forgotten that dedicated women had followed Jesus about and '*deaconed*' for Him. Indeed, the place of women in early Christianity is in striking contrast to anything to be found in other religions. Christians not only proclaimed that in Christ 'there is neither male nor female' (Gal. 3: 28); they acted upon it. It was to women that Jesus entrusted the first tidings of His Resurrection (Mt. 28: 7). The women are next seen at prayer with the apostles (Acts 1: 14), waiting for the promised outpouring of the Spirit on sons and daughters alike (Acts 2: 17). We find them owning houses which they use for Christian worship (Acts 12: 12); we find them, with their husbands, selling property (Acts 5: 1). We find them engaged in Christian work, women like Mary, Tryphaena and

Tryphosa who 'labour in the Lord' (Rom. 16: 6, 12). We find them associated with Paul in spreading the Gospel (Phil. 4: 3), and it is hard to imagine that this did not sometimes include preaching. Certainly Priscilla seems to have been a women of remarkable gifts who so eclipsed her husband that four times out of the six that they are jointly mentioned her name stands first! It was she, as well as her husband Aquila, who gave Apollos his early instruction in the Christian faith (Acts 18: 26). No doubt preaching, at all events to a mixed congregation, was not usually one of their tasks, though despite Paul's disapproval (I Tim. 2: 11–13) it must on occasion have happened. What are we to make, otherwise, of the four prophesying daughters of Philip? In the Corinthian church women were abusing the new freedom that they found in the Gospel, and not only prayed and prophesied at the meetings for worship (I Cor. 11: 5), but also spoke in tongues (I Cor. 14: 34 in context). Speaking in tongues can be controlled (14: 27), and so women are forbidden to use this gift in public, for if male glossolalia leads to disorder, female glossolalia leads to chaos, as the Irvingite movement discovered. But prophecy is a different matter, so is prayer. So Paul merely insists that when a woman is exercising these gifts in the assembly she should be properly veiled, as the decencies of the time dictated (11: 1–15). She is certainly not relegated to a merely passive role in the conduct of public worship. This is a point of some consequence in these days when the ministry of women is being considered anew. Scripture makes it plain, however, that theirs is, like the male diaconate, an auxiliary ministry. The woman shares a community of life with the man, but has a different and subordinate function; precisely the same holds good of man's relationship with God (I Cor. 11:3). The man is head of the family unit; it is his responsibility to lead, not hers (I Cor. 11:3; Eph. 5:22 ff.). The woman's normal place is not in the pulpit but in the home (I Tim. 2:11–15). And through woman's gossiping of the Gospel in the home, at the laundry, and to her friends, quite as much as through formal preaching by the man, the Christian message pervaded the ancient world.

The diaconate of women has indeed been restored in the Anglican Communion for over half a century now, but its possibilities have not yet been fully explored, nor its challenge laid before girls in the same way as ordination has been held up before boys. It is only on the mission field that the woman worker really comes into her own, and even there it is largely because of the lack of men. The New Testament lays before us an ideal of *diakonia* in which women engage as fully as men. The Church of the Servant must not neglect this pattern; it cannot afford to.

CHAPTER SIX

BARRIERS TO REUNION—
APOSTOLIC SUCCESSION

THE Ecumenical Movement is the most remarkable development in the Church of the twentieth century. Everywhere churches are looking towards reunion. There are, however, two elements in the doctrine of the ministry which are proving serious barriers to reunion. They have been spotlighted in the Anglican-Methodist Report; they lurk like submerged icebergs in the Anglican-Presbyterian Conversations at present in progress. They are, of course, apostolic succession and sacrificial priesthood. We shall examine apostolic succession in this chapter, and priesthood in the next.

A. THE PLACE OF THE APOSTLES IN THE CHURCH

The word 'apostle' is so loosely used in current talk about 'apostolic orders', 'apostolic delegates', 'the apostolate of the laity', and the like, that it may be profitable to glance briefly at the place the apostles occupied in the early Church. This is not at all easy, for there are many questions to which we do not know the answer. We do not know how many they were; we have almost no hint as to what they did after the early chapters of Acts, where, in any case, only Peter and John are prominent. We do not know for certain that a woman might not have been an apostle! Romans 16: 7 may be translated 'Andronicus and *Junia* . . . who are of note among the apostles'. C. H. Dodd in his *Moffatt Commentary* refers to Chrysostom's homily on the subject and says drily: 'Chrysostom, preaching on this passage, saw no difficulty in a woman-apostle; nor need we.'[1] Most important of all, we do not know for certain that the apostles had much to do with ordination and the administration of the sacraments. As far as the latter goes, we know that

[1] P. 239. There are, of course, other ways of explaining this verse!

Paul was not in the habit of baptizing (I Cor. 1: 14), and there is no actual evidence that they normally presided at celebrations of the holy communion. Certainly there is not a hint that a 'valid' communion could not be had without the imposition of their hands upon the celebrant. As a matter of fact, the New Testament evidence that the apostles made a habit of ordaining is far from conclusive. Thus Eduard Schweizer says: 'We have seen Paul does not know ordination . . . there is in the churches of which he has the care no rite by which people are either installed or ordained for particular ministries, and that it would be impossible for him to regard any such rite otherwise than as a subsequent recognition of a ministry which had been bestowed previously. The same is true of John's Gospel and Letters. Thus in the New Testament there were large sections of the Church where no special action was performed to assign a special ministry.'[2] W. Telfer finds in the New Testament 'no evidence that presbyter-bishops could only become such by apostolic appointment, or that, when appointed, they received a laying on of apostolic hands';[3] and A. T. Hanson, in commenting on the view that the apostles took steps for the preservation of the ministry, asks: 'What steps did they take? Except for Paul, the only possible way in which the ministry could have been described as being perpetuated was in the presbyters of the Jerusalem church in Acts. But to describe these presbyters as successors of the apostles is absolutely fatal to the "Catholic" theory of the ministry. That is why everyone who tries to find evidence for the "Catholic" theory has to invent or discover a set of bishops (who were also called presbyters) to carry on the essential succession from the apostles to the bishops of the second century'.[4]

One final difficulty is that the word 'apostle' appears to have been used to denote two different categories of people in the early Church. The word means 'sent', and was so applied to special delegates sent out from a church (II Cor. 8: 23; Phil. 2: 25; Acts 14: 4, 14; and often in the *Didache*). But it was, of course, used, *par excellence*, of the apostles of Jesus Christ, and it is with them that we are concerned.

The title is conferred only sparingly on the Twelve during

[2] *Op. cit.*, p. 207.
[3] *The Office of a Bishop*, p. 41.
[4] *The Pioneer Ministry*, p. 144.

59

the ministry of Jesus. They were called primarily that they might be with Him, and secondarily that He might send them forth to preach, heal and exorcize (Mk. 3: 14, 15). They are represented throughout the ministry as learners, 'disciples'. They will be 'apostles' later, when their Master is no longer with them. This, indeed, happens in the Book of Acts, where 'apostles' is their constant title, and that of 'disciples' disappears. In just one place in his Gospel Mark gives them the title 'apostles', and it is, significantly, when they return from the mission of preaching and healing on which Jesus has sent them (Mk. 6: 30). Matthew also only uses the word of the disciples on this mission (10: 2 ff.), and gives us a very clear idea of what apostleship meant. For they go forth clothed with His authority to do His work. Their message is His message, to preach that the kingdom of heaven is at hand (v. 7). Their function is His function, to be the Servant of the Lord and heal the sick, cleanse the lepers, raise the dead, cast out devils (v. 8). It is precisely the same programme that He Himself fulfils in His message to John the Baptist (11: 5): 'The blind receive their sight and the lame walk, lepers are cleansed and the deaf hear, and the dead are raised up, and the poor have good news preached to them.' They are to be His representatives plenipotentiary—'whosoever receiveth you receiveth me' (10: 40); and here we are given a miniature of the apostolic mission as it would develop after the resurrection. Meanwhile their task is to be with Him, and to get to know Him whom later they would represent. So as soon as they return from this mission they become 'disciples' again, and so they remain until the end of the book.

After the resurrection the apostolic band takes the place of Jesus (Mt. 28: 18–20; Acts 1: 8). They are to become witnesses to Jesus, as He was to the Father, and the Spirit will bear witness, too (Jn. 15: 26, 27). They will be led by that same Spirit into all the truth about Jesus, and become the authoritative interpreters of the person and work of Jesus (Jn. 14: 26; 16: 13–15). Thus the apostles become the norm of doctrine in the early Church (Acts 2: 42). 'That is why,' writes Cullmann, 'the New Testament attributes the same images to Jesus as to the apostles: "rocks" and the corresponding images of "foundation", "pillars". Never are these images used to designate the bishop.'[5] So closely are they integrated with the

[5] *Christianity Divided*, Sheen & Ward (1961), p. 10.

60

person of their Master that Cullmann can say with truth: 'The Apostolate does not belong to the period of the Church, but to that of the Incarnation of Christ.'[6] Indeed, so close is the identity between the Sender and the sent that the New Testament can regard the apostolic tradition and teaching about Jesus as from the Lord Himself.[7] The exalted Lord proclaims through His apostles His own teaching and the extension of what He had said while He was on earth. Then it was a case of having many things to say to them which, at the time, they were not able to assimilate.

Since Pentecost, however, the Holy Spirit has actualized for the apostles the mind of the Lord Jesus (I Cor. 2:16), as He Himself promised: 'When the Spirit of truth comes, He will guide you into all the truth, for He will not speak on His own authority . . . He will glorify me, for He will take what is mine and declare it to you' (Jn. 16: 13, 14); and again: 'The Holy Spirit whom the Father will send in my name, He will teach you [that is, you apostles] all things, and bring to your remembrance all that I have said to you' (Jn. 14: 26). As A. F. Walls succinctly puts it: 'This witness, being grounded in a unique experience of the incarnate Christ, and directed by a special dispensation of the Holy Spirit, provides the authentic interpretation of Christ, and has ever since been determinative for the universal Church. In the nature of things the office could not be repeated or transmitted; any more than the underlying historic experiences could be transmitted to those who had never known the incarnate Lord or received a resurrection appearance.'[8]

This unique teaching office, springing from the fact that their witness to Jesus was *direct*, while all other witness is *derived* (or, as Paul puts it in Gal. 1: 1–12, their reception of the Gospel was *di'apokalypseos*, by revelation, not *di'anthropou*, through human intermediaries), sets the apostles apart, and this fact was recognized by the second-century Church when they took care to admit to the canon only those writings which they knew emanated from the apostolic circle. Through the

[6] *Op. cit.*, p. 10.
[7] See Cullmann's essay 'The Tradition' in his book *The Early Church*, S.C.M. (1956), and on the supreme teaching office of the apostles, N. Geldenhuys' *Supreme Authority*, M.M.S. (1953).
[8] Article 'Apostle' in the *New Bible Dictionary*, I.V.F. (1962).

61

witness of the apostolic band[9] the first-century world was enabled to encounter Jesus; through their witness, recorded in the Scriptures of the New Testament, twentieth-century men can still meet their Lord. And just as the early Church was bound by the apostolic witness both for doctrine and behaviour,[10] so is the Church of subsequent ages. We are bound to the apostles and their testimony; we cannot get behind them. We believe because of their word (Jn. 17: 20). This is the apostolic succession that was envisaged by Jesus. The apostles are, in fact, historically unique and doctrinally normative.

But in other respects, of course, the apostles do have successors. As missionaries, as preachers, as servants of the Lord, as ministers of the Gospel and the sacraments, as leaders of the Christian community, they have successors. The question is, wherein does this succession lie?

B. THE SUCCESSION TO THE APOSTLES IN THE CHURCH

Apostolic succession is a phrase with several meanings. It can refer to doctrinal succession whereby later generations recognize that they are bound by the teachings of the founder-members of the Church, the apostles who were themselves taught by Jesus.

The phrase is also applied to a succession of function and authority. It was used in this sense by Irenaeus and Hippolytus at the end of the second century to describe the succession of one bishop to another in a see. This succession was a valuable guardian of the apostolic faith, especially in the days when Gnostic error was encroaching on the Church, and when the canon of apostolic writings was not yet clearly defined. Indeed, through such a succession of bishops in their sees the Church at large learnt to express its conviction that the ministry is one

---

[9] It was a corporate witness, not the perquisite of any one individual. The homogeneity of this witness, and the extent to which it underlies every stratum of the New Testament, have been shewn in C. H. Dodd's books *The Apostolic Preaching and its Development*, Hodder and Stoughton (1936) and *According to the Scriptures*, Nisbet (1952).

[10] I Tim. 6: 3–5; II Thess. 3: 14; II Jn. 10; and supremely I Cor. 14: 37 f.: 'If any one does not recognize this (that what I am writing to you is a commandment of the Lord), he is not recognized.'

throughout the world and down the ages. It is, therefore, reasonable to expect that in the future reunited Church of God episcopacy will have an important and expressive part to play.

It is with the third interpretation of 'apostolic succession' that violent disagreement sets in. This view claims that the apostles ordained the bishops to succeed them, and that the historic episcopate, stretching in unbroken succession back to the apostles, is essential to the Church. Without such ordination it is impossible to exercise a 'valid' ministry or celebrate a 'valid' sacrament.

This view has occasionally been found in individual Anglican writers since the Reformation, but it came to the fore only last century with Newman's first *Tract for the Times* at the beginning of the Oxford Movement. The traditional exposition of the doctrine from then on has been that the threefold ministry is a divine institution stemming from the apostles and secured by an unbroken line of ordinations. The publication of *The Apostolic Ministry* in 1946, however, gave a new turn to the argument. It divided ministries into *essential* (that is, that possessed by the episcopate, in succession to the apostles) and *dependent* (that is, all other ministries). Such a doctrine was flattering to the bishops, and seems to have strengthened the current ecclesiastical tendency towards the separation of the bishops from the presbyters, but it was very damaging to the old 'catholic' dogma of the threefold ministry.

Dix goes so far as to say that all this talk about the historic episcopate is beside the point. He recognizes that the nonconformist ministries should not be offered *episkope*, for they already possess it. Indeed, in one respect they are more entitled than the Anglicans to the title of *episkopoi*, for their ministers are freely chosen by their own churches, in contrast to Anglican bishops who are nominees of the state (p. 295 f.). 'What is really in question in our present discussions about "episcopacy" is not the "episcopate" at all. It is the "apostolate".' Dix is not interested in the pros and cons of the concentration of *episkope* in the hands of a single individual; this is unimportant and could be disastrous, as the New Testament precedent of Diotrephes shows. (He, of course, of all figures in the New Testament acts most like a later monarchical bishop, and is condemned in the most uncompromising terms

63

in III John.) No, Dix, together with Kirk in the introductory essay, argues that the essence of apostolic authority is its derivation from the Lord. The principle is plain, 'as the Father has sent me, even so send I you'. This commission from Jesus the apostles passed on to the bishops who are the custodians of it today.

That is the theory in its essentials; and in order to bolster it up, Dix propounds, and Kirk accepts, the doctrine of the Jewish *shaliach*. This officer figures a good deal in rabbinic writings. He is a delegate with plenipotentiary powers; thus 'he that is sent is as he that sent him.' There is indeed some evidence to suggest that such a view as this underlay the idea of apostle, as Rengstorf has shewn.[11] It would account very well, for one thing, for the unique authority of the apostles to which the second-century Church wistfully looked back. It is not conclusive evidence, however. For one thing, the *shaliach* always acted within Judaism and had no missionary function, which was the main *raison d'être* of the apostles. More serious still, there is little evidence to suggest that the idea of *shaliach* had arisen in Judaism by the first century A.D. But what is so damaging for the whole theory, as T. W. Manson, L. Morris and A. Ehrhardt[12] have pointed out with devastating clarity, is that the *shaliach* could *not transmit his authority*. 'We are therefore forced to conclude', writes Dr. Ehrhardt, 'that unless Dr. Kirk abandons Rengstorf's theory that the apostle was the *shaliach* of Christ, he cannot very well maintain the doctrine of apostolic succession' (p. 20). It should be noted that this criticism comes from one who is sympathetic to the doctrine in some form, and so unsatisfactory does he find the attempt of the *Apostolic Ministry* to demonstrate this succession in the early period, that he writes his book to try and prove it another way, by means of a priestly succession through James of Jerusalem—an attempt which must be adjudged no more successful.

There is, therefore, considerable confusion in the arguments with which the Anglo-Catholic position has been supported

---

[11] See his article 'Apostleship' in Kittel's *Theol. Wörterbuch zum Neuen Testament*, translated in A. and C. Black's *Kittel Bible Key Words* (1952).

[12] T. W. Manson: *The Church's Ministry*, pp. 35–52; A. Ehrhardt: *The Apostolic Succession*, chapter I, and L. Morris: *Ministers of God*, pp. 114–118.

in recent years,[13] and it is probably true to say that only a small minority in the Church of England accept it. Nevertheless, it is a vociferous and influential minority, and so it may be as well to ask four questions of this theory. Is it the biblical teaching ? Is it sound theology ? Is it historically demonstrable ? Is it Anglican doctrine ?

1. *Is it the biblical teaching ?*

The Church of England takes its stand fairly and squarely on the supremacy and sufficiency of Scripture. Article VI declares explicitly that 'Holy Scripture containeth all things necessary to salvation, so that whatsoever is not read therein, nor may be proved thereby, is not to be required of any man, that it should be believed as an article of the Faith, or be thought requisite or necessary to salvation'.

Nobody has yet succeeded in demonstrating that apostolic succession is taught in Scripture, certainly not the authors of *The Apostolic Ministry*, where a great deal of special pleading is supported by such expedients as typology and rabbinic

---

[13] Indeed, an example of even greater confusion—or is it the beginning of a new attitude among Anglo-Catholics ?—is to be found in an article in the Kelham magazine, *S.S.M.* for March 1964 by Gilbert Sinden. He abandons the identification of apostle and *shaliach* because of the fatal objection that 'a *shaliach* cannot pass on his authority to someone else (cf. *Gittin* 3 : 6)', and recognizes that 'the Twelve were regarded as a once-for-all body within the Church; the "apostles of the churches" were occasional officials and in no sense "successors" of the Twelve'. Earlier in his article he had already rejected Dix's notion that the episcopate was regarded as the same office as the apostolate in the New Testament and the early Church. His conclusion is that 'the Church herself was apostolic, "sent" by the Father as Jesus had been "sent" by the Father . . . So far as the New Testament is concerned, there is no suggestion that Jesus, or the Twelve, had instituted a ministry of bishops, priests and deacons, but the New Testament is very clear that the Church's very nature is to exercise pastoral care (*episkope*), priesthood—and especially an evangelistic priesthood of the Gospel (*hierosyne*), and service of all kinds (*diakonia*) both to its own members and to the world at large for whom Christ had died. These are the marks of the Church, and it was only natural and proper that its organization should reflect its nature.' If this really is the latest Anglo-Catholic position, it is precisely that advocated by the Free Churchman, Professor T. W. Manson, in chapters 2 and 3 of his book *The Church's Ministry*, and while boding well for future inter-church relations, makes current Anglican intransigence over the necessity of episcopal ordination look particularly dated.

precedents. It is true that the 'apostles'[14] Paul and Barnabas are once represented as appointing presbyters in every town. Very likely it was their regular practice, doubtless with the laying on of hands with prayer. But we are never told that the apostles had hands laid on them by our Lord. We are never told that the ministry in all Christian communities had to wait for an apostle to come and authorize it. Indeed, the New Testament indications, quite as much as the probabilities of the case, suggest that the first ministers in any congregation were appointed by the missionaries (often relatively unknown folk, see Acts 8: 1–4; 11: 19–26), and then became self-recruiting. There was certainly a ministry in Rome and Antioch before these cities were visited by any apostle, and it is interesting to note that when Paul left Philippi after his first visit there was only a tiny group of believers and no hint of any regular ministry (Acts 16), whilst when he came to write to the Philippians a few years later (without having visited them in the meantime), there is a flourishing ministry of bishops and deacons (1: 1). There is, in fact, no suggestion that apostolic commissioning was indispensable for the ministry; to think in these terms is an anachronism. Not until early in the third century did the doctrine of manual transmission of the grace of orders begin to arise.[15]

Furthermore, the holders of this view fail consistently to recognize the fact that there was a diversity of practice in New Testament times, and that 'primitive catholic uniformity' is nothing but a romantic myth. Karl Holl and Eduard Schweizer[16] in influential books (entirely neglected by the authors of *The Apostolic Ministry*) have shewn that there is a diversity of practice in the New Testament itself. The prototype of 'catholic order' is represented by James and the Jewish church; the second-century episcopal lists mostly claimed to reach back to him.

The Pauline churches, on the other hand, are interested in

[14] Paul and Barnabas are only called 'apostles' in the Acts in chapter 14, when they are delegates of the Antioch church (13: 1–5 cf. 14: 26–28). We do not know whether Barnabas was an 'Apostle of Jesus Christ'.

[15] This is recognized by Dix, *op. cit.*, pp. 200 f.

[16] K. Holl: *Gesammelte Werke* 11, pp. 44 f., and E. Schweizer: *Das Leben des Herrn in der Gemeinde und ihren Diensten*, Zurich, 1946.

order but not in succession.[17] Paul himself was called in no succession; no one laid ordaining hands on him, and he is clear that anyone, however impeccable his ministerial pedigree, must be judged by his faithfulness to the Gospel message (Gal. 1: 8). After all, Judas was an apostle. He too has had a succession in the history of the Church!

There is discernible a third attitude to church order in the New Testament, that of the Johannine writings, where there are no offices as such, no special ministries, even the word 'apostle' has disappeared; the gift of the Spirit, and the believer's direct union with God and love for the brethren take their place.[18]

Even if there were not this variety within the church order of the New Testament itself, the silence of Scripture would be decisive. If episcopacy were essential to the Church, God would have made it quite clear to us. Would the God who attested the certainty of our forgiveness by the resurrection leave us with no clear direction as to church order, had it been necessary for man's salvation, as this theory asserts?

2. *Is it sound theology?*

The strength of the view we are considering is that it takes very seriously the visible Church of God as the society which, for all its faults, Jesus left to carry on His work in the world. But such an approach is exposed to several dangers.

It tends to limit the grace of God to episcopal communions, and regards with grudging reluctance the evidence, which is plain for all to see, that He works just as effectively in non-episcopal churches. It simply will not do to dismiss this evidence with talk of 'uncovenanted mercies' and the like.

Secondly, such a view is in great danger of depersonalizing the grace of God; instead of the loving relation of the Father to His child, grace becomes a commodity which may only be obtained through the proper channels. This is a serious declension from the New Testament concept of the grace of God.[19]

Thirdly, this view tends to regard the grace of God and the

[17] No later churches drew succession lists from a ministry ordained by Paul or his lieutenants Timothy and Titus.
[18] See Schweizer: *Church Order in the New Testament*, pp. 117–130.
[19] See Brunner's passionate protest against such depersonalization in his *Misunderstanding of the Church*.

working of His Spirit as something that can be organized and controlled. Once you start thinking, as the authors of *The Apostolic Ministry* avowedly think, of those in the apostolic succession as 'plenipotentiaries' of Christ, you fall little short of blasphemy against the Holy Spirit, Christ's true 'plenipotentiary'.[20] It is, no doubt, very comfortable, but entirely false, to think that the external form inevitably carries with it the internal grace. God remains sovereign in His working. No system of dogmatics, no method of church order can get Him 'taped'. Catholicism runs the same danger as did Judaism, of forgetting that the Church stands or falls by the response of faith to grace — and not by a succession. The Jews felt they had something (the Law), by keeping which they could exert a claim on God. The whole New Testament gives the lie to any such claim on the part of men, and yet the doctrine of apostolic succession comes perilously near to reasserting it. As Bishop Robinson emphasizes in his essay on the subject, the Church is not the Kingdom; it always remains subject both to the kingly rule and the judgment of God: 'To claim that the Church now has "the plenitude" is to forget that. Ecclesiasticism is always in danger of subordinating both the spiritual and the eschatological to the historical.'[21]

One other point is important. This doctrine of apostolic succession reverses the New Testament picture of a ministry dependent upon the Church. Instead we are presented with a Church so dependent upon the ministry that if, as could well have happened at some periods of church history, such as the Diocletian persecution, all Christian ministers standing in the supposed succession had been rounded up and killed, that would have been the end of the Church. Such a view, of course, borders on fantasy, but what else can Bishop Kirk mean when he says, 'should such a ministry (that is, the "essential ministry" of bishops in the succession) fail, the apostolic Church, which is the Body of Christ in space and

[20] Indeed, both those who accept and those who reject this doctrine of apostolic succession recognize that in the last analysis they have a different conception of *God*. Thus Bishop Stephen Neill 'cannot recognize as Christian the doctrine of God' underlying *The Apostolic Ministry* (*The Ministry of the Church*, p. 28), while Bishop Kirk (*The Apostolic Ministry*, p. 32) admits: 'In the end these [different doctrines of the ministry] will be discovered to involve divergent beliefs about the nature of God Himself.'

[21] *The Historic Episcopate*, pp. 18 f.

time, would disappear with it (for the two are inextricably bound together)²² ? But according to the New Testament, the fullness of the Godhead, which indwelt the incarnate Christ, now dwells in all Christians corporately (Col. 2: 9, 10; Eph. 1: 23), not in any ministerial *élite*. The ministry, like all the other members in Christ's Body, exists for the sake of the Body (Eph. 4: 11–14; Col. 1: 24, 25). It exists to build up the saints for the work of ministry (Eph. 4: 12). For it is not merely the ordained ministry but the whole Church which has inherited the apostolic commission, 'Go and make disciples of all nations, baptizing them . . . teaching them to observe all that I have commanded you; and lo, I am with you always, to the close of the age' (Mt. 28: 19 f.). The whole Church succeeds to the apostolic charge because she is called, empowered, instructed and sent by Christ to go and make disciples of the nations.

3. *Is it historically demonstrable?*

Once again the answer must be 'No'. Ignatius holds an immensely high doctrine of episcopacy, but he has not a word to say about any supposed succession from the apostles. Indeed, he goes to some lengths to dissociate himself from them; thus: 'I do not command you, as Peter and Paul did. They were apostles, I am a convict' (*Rom.* 4, cf. *Trall.* 1). The *Didache*, furthermore, which enjoyed vast prestige in the early Church, enjoins on the congregations to which it writes the necessity of their *appointing their own bishops and deacons* (15: 1)! Clement of Rome knows that—at Corinth—the apostles appointed bishops (44: 1) or presbyters (44: 5) 'with a further enactment that if they should fall asleep other approved men should succeed to their ministry'. It is perverse to make the 'their' refer to the apostles; it clearly refers to the deceased bishops, and we have, therefore, in Clement a corporate succession in office which is the precursor of the monarchical succession to be found first in Irenaeus and Hegesippus at the end of the second century. These writers still have not any doctrine of manual transmission of grace. Irenaeus, it now seems almost certain, was consecrated not by another bishop but by the council of his presbyters in Lugdunum.²³ This practice of presbyteral consecration continued

²² *The Apostolic Ministry*, p. 40.
²³ See E. Molland: *Journal of Ecclesiastical History* (1950), i, pp. 12–28.

until the fourth century in Alexandria.[24] The doctrine of the manual transmission of grace for episcopacy in succession from the apostles is first found in third-century Latin Christians. It is interesting, as T. M. Lindsay points out, to note that many of its inventors were lawyers, men like Cyprian, Tertullian and Augustine. 'Apostolic succession in the dogmatic sense', he says, 'is the legal fiction required by the legal mind to connect the growing conceptions of the authority of the clergy with the earlier days of Christianity. It served the Christian lawyer in much the same way that another curious legal fiction assisted the pagan civilian. The latter insisted that the government of the Emperors from Augustus to Diocletian was the prolongation of the old Republican constitution; the former imagined that the rule of bishops was the prolongation through the generations of the inspired guidance of the original apostles who were the planters of the Church.'[25] So much for a Presbyterian summary of the situation, written fifty years ago. The Anglican church historian, Dr. Telfer, who has contributed the most recent review of the evidence, agrees. 'These Latin churchmen created a historical myth, the unhistorical nature of which they were secure from discovering. This was to the effect that the apostles had provided for the future of the Church by creating an order of monarchical bishops. The first of these they ordained, according to this myth, with their own hands, and set them to govern the several churches with which they were concerned.'[26]

4. Is it Anglican doctrine?

In the first place, it is important to remember that the Church of England requires no one to believe as necessary any doctrine which cannot be proved from Scripture (Art. VI). This doctrine of apostolic succession in the third sense defined above (p. 63) cannot be so proved, and therefore we would expect to find nothing in the formularies of the Church of England to require its acceptance. That is precisely what we do find. Succession is not included in the marks of the Church (Art. XIX); it is not mentioned in Art. XXIII which deals with the subject of ministering in the congregation; and the Preface to the Ordinal carefully refrains from unchurching non-episcopal

[24] See E. W. Kemp: *Journal of Ecclesiastical History* (1955), vi, pp. 125–142; see also W. Telfer: *J.E.H.* (1952), iii, pp. 1–13.
[25] *The Church and the Ministry in the Early Centuries*, p. 279.
[26] *The Office of a Bishop*, p. 119.

bodies, while giving good grounds for the retention of the threefold ministry in our own church. A sentence from the Preface to the Prayer Book is relevant here: 'In these our doings we condemn no other nations, nor prescribe anything but to our own people only.' Furthermore, the Church of England explicitly claims to uphold the doctrine of justification by faith only (Art. XI); in other words she unashamedly takes her stand with the churches of the Reformation on this issue which divided Christendom in the sixteenth century. This does not mean for one moment, as Dix rather loosely asserts, that 'where the doctrine of "Justification by faith alone" is held, no question of church order can be anything but entirely secondary, even meaningless' (*op. cit.*, p. 301), but it assuredly does mean that where this doctrine is held, no one form of the ministry should be or can be regarded as essential for the existence of the Church. Presbyterians, for instance, have the highest regard for the importance of regular and public succession to the ministry, and yet hold jealously to the doctrine of justification. They ground the validity of their succession not so much in historical continuity (to do so would be to have 'confidence in the flesh', Phil. 3: 3), but in the promise of Christ to be with the Church down the ages. 'Ministerial succession in no way secures the possession of the Holy Spirit, nor does it guarantee a lawful ministry. But because it is the apostolically appointed ordinance, it cannot be condemned or neglected without disobedience and loss.'[27]

This seems to me to be not only the spiritually healthy attitude to succession, but the one that has been most characteristic of the Church of England since the Reformation. The Reformers themselves freely intercommunicated with their brethren in the Reformed and Lutheran Churches on the Continent; this practice continued for over 200 years. Bishop Joseph Hall, who in 1618 attended the Synod of Dort as a representative of the Church of England, could write in his book *Peacemaker* on his return: 'There is no difference in any essential matter betwixt the Church of England and her sisters of the Reformation. We accord in every point of Christian doctrine, without the least variation.'[28]

[27] *Manual of Church Doctrine according to the Church of Scotland*, ed. Torrance and Selby Wright, p. 98.

[28] Quoted by N. Sykes: *The Church of England and Non-Episcopal Churches*, p. 23.

Richard Hooker, that most representative of Anglicans, prized episcopacy very highly, and yet refused to conclude that it is absolutely necessary. He gives as one exception, 'when God Himself doth of Himself raise up any, whose labour He useth without requiring that men should authorize them'; as another, 'when necessity doth constrain to leave the usual ways of the Church which otherwise we would willingly keep' (*Eccl. Pol.* VII, xiv, 11). This was the situation which forced Luther to break with Rome. The papacy of his day would allow no appeal from itself to Scripture. Luther had to choose between sound doctrine and episcopal consecration. As R. F. Hettlinger justly observes: 'The Lutherans were ready to preserve unity even if the bishops personally rejected their doctrines, so long as they would ordain men who believed in justification by faith, but "they admit none except they will swear not to teach the pure doctrine of the Gospel" (Augsburg Confession of 1530)'.[29] Hooker himself concluded that 'the Church hath power by universal consent to take it [episcopacy] away, if thereunto she be constrained through the proud, tyrannical, and unreformable dealings of her bishops' (*op. cit.* VII, v, 8). Episcopacy, though valuable, is not indispensable.

The late Professor Norman Sykes has shown in two influential books, *Old Priest and New Presbyter* and *The Church of England and Non-Episcopal Churches in the Sixteenth and Seventeenth Centuries* that this was the characteristic Anglican position, including most of the high church Caroline divines, until the Oxford Movement, when in the first of the celebrated *Tracts for the Times* Newman wrote of the bishop in ordination that 'he but *transmits*; and thus the Christian Ministry is a *succession*. And if we trace back the power of ordination from hand to hand, of course, we shall come to the Apostles at last. We know we do, as a plain historical fact (!) . . . We must necessarily consider none to be *really* ordained unless they have been *thus* ordained'. The Anglo-Catholic doctrine of the *exclusive* validity of those orders which come within the apostolic succession was something quite novel in the Church of England.[30] It is not doctrinally sound, scripturally based, historically reputable, or part of the teaching of our Church. Indeed, the Anglo-Catholic historian Darwell Stone admits

[29] *Episcopacy and Reunion*, Mowbray (1953), p. 81.
[30] See the evidence set out in J. W. Hunkins, *Episcopal Ordination and Confirmation in relation to Inter-Communion and Reunion.*

72

that it is impossible to argue 'that the present formularies and the post-Reformation English divines are committed to the necessity of episcopal ordination as distinct from the practical requirement in the Church of England'.[31]

In view of this, it seems astonishing that this dogma of apostolic succession should be allowed to bedevil the promising conversations at present in progress with a view to reuniting the Protestant churches in these islands. Anything done here would give a great impetus to such reunions elsewhere in the world. The Church of England may quite properly ask that those with whom she enters into union shall accept the fact, without any 'particular theory or interpretation',[32] of episcopacy from then onwards. It would, however, be a gross impropriety to stipulate that those ministers entering the united church shall be episcopally ordained. Time and time again Anglicans have been thought muddled or, what is worse, insincere, because despite repeated protestations such as the Lambeth Appeal of 1920 (which spoke of the 'spiritual reality of Free Church ministries'[33]), and the Memorandum of the Joint Conference which followed it (and which so far from finding Free Church ministries 'invalid, that is null and void', declared, 'we regard them as being within their several spheres real ministries in the Universal Church'[34]), there has, nevertheless, been a marked unwillingness to admit the churches concerned to communion without the explicit or implicit reordination of their ministers.

'The challenge of the single successful experiment in reunion from the Church of South India,' wrote Sykes,[35] 'and the contrast between its unequivocal taking of episcopacy into its system, and the equivocal response of Lambeth 1948, have

[31] Quoted in N. Sykes: *Old Priest and New Presbyter*, p. 212.
[32] *Lambeth Conference Report* (1930).
[33] 'We do not call in question for a moment the spiritual reality of the ministries of those communions which do not possess the Episcopate. On the contrary, we thankfully acknowledge that these ministries have been manifestly blessed and owned by the Holy Spirit as effective means of grace' (*Lambeth Report* (1920), 9.7).
[34] See G. K. A. Bell: *Documents on Christian Unity* (1924), p. 158. As R. F. Hettlinger comments (*op. cit.*, p. 95), Bishop Kirk recognizes the unpalatable fact that this Memorandum gives away the Anglo-Catholic case, and therefore devoted two pages to showing that it is patient of another legitimate interpretation (see Kirk: *op. cit.*, pp. 42–45).
[35] *Old Priest and New Presbyter*, pp. 237 f.

raised . . . the query whether from the Anglican side episcopacy has not assumed the elusive characteristic of the ghost of Hamlet's father "*Hic et ubique*: then we'll shift our ground". The differences between Lambeth in 1930 and in 1948 have evoked the suspicion that in fact a particular interpretation of the historic episcopate (and not the adoption of that institution alone) is being asked of non-episcopal churches as a condition of full union or intercommunion; and, further, that this interpretation is not the traditional Anglican doctrine of episcopacy but the exclusive theory of Tractarian *provenance* and championship.'

It is very much to be hoped that the next Lambeth Conference will reassert the truth that the Church of England has never held episcopacy to be of the *esse* of the Church, and that the widespread assumption among our nonconformist brethren that this is the official Anglican doctrine, is a misconception, unsupported by Scripture, our formularies, or our historical practice. In fact, more than once in our history (notably between 1610 and 1638 in our relations with Scots when episcopalians did not reordain those whom presbyterians had already ordained, and later for many years in India[36]) there have coexisted for a period after union two types of ministry, those episcopally and those not episcopally ordained. It is tragic that these precedents were not, apparently, known to the Lambeth Bishops in 1948 who said, in defence of their equivocal attitude to the Church of South India: 'We have never yet entered into full communion with any church which does not possess a fully unified ministry, episcopally ordained.' It would be more tragic still if the prospect of reunion with the Methodists and Presbyterians were marred by similar intransigence upon this point.

While it is right to respect the views of minorities as far as possible, *is* it right that a view which was introduced into Anglicanism with the Tractarians, a view which led their most consistent thinkers to join the Church of Rome, should be allowed to prejudice the reunion of the Anglican Church with some of her sister churches of the Reformation? And if it be argued that reunion with these churches on these terms would

[36] See Bishop Stephen Neill in *The Ministry of the Church*, p. 21, and Sykes: *op. cit.*, p. 236, also G. E. Duffield's article 'Intercommunion and the Ministry', in *The Churchman*, December 1963, pp. 235 ff.

prejudice our eventual reunion with Rome and the Orthodox Church,[37] this must be resisted; for these churches do not believe that our orders are valid in any case! They do not accept that we have the precious gift which we are so anxious to pass on to others. So reunion with other Reformation churches is unlikely to alter our future relations with Rome. There is great value in a bridge, provided it reaches both sides of the gulf. But there is not much value in a 'bridge church', as the Church of England delights to be, if it fails to reach either side. And that is precisely the danger that the Church of England has been running since the Tractarian Movement alienated us from the Reformed churches without gaining for us recognition from the 'Catholic' side.

[37] For the rather complex evidence on Orthodox views of Anglican orders, see T. Ware: *The Orthodox Church*, pp. 324 ff.

CHAPTER SEVEN

BARRIERS TO REUNION—SACRIFICIAL PRIESTHOOD

As we saw in an earlier chapter, the word 'priest' is derived in terms both of etymology and function from the 'elder' (Greek *presbyteros*) of the New Testament. There is, however, another meaning commonly associated with the word—one who offers sacrifice. The Greek word for such a person is quite distinct, *hiereus*, a sacrificing priest. This is not a mere matter of playing with words. The meaning is important for the whole conception of the Christian ministry. Calvin complained of the Roman Catholic bishops that 'by their ordination they create not presbyters to rule and feed the people, but priests to offer sacrifice'. Does the Church of England do this? The answer which appears increasingly to underlie modern Anglican pronouncements is 'Yes'. The idea is that the priest, duly ordained in the apostolic succession, has entrusted to him the authority and power to offer the sacrifice of the eucharist. It is of this that the Minority Report in the Anglican-Methodist Conversations complains (p. 60): 'Whatever the etymology of the English word *priest*, in this report it means more than *presbyter*. It is expressly connected with sacrificial views of the Eucharist.' Because this conception of the priesthood in the Church of England is undoubtedly a grave barrier to any hopes of reunion, we must examine both the New Testament evidence and the historic position of the Church of England.

A. PRIESTHOOD AND SACRIFICE IN THE NEW TESTAMENT

1. *The Priesthood of Christ and His Sacrifice*

I do not think that it is necessary these days to go over much of the old ground again. It is recognized on all sides now that Christ sums up in Himself all that was symbolized by the sacrificing priesthood of the Old Testament. He has Himself so discharged the office of a *hiereus* that no other priest is needed, and no needs of the human soul remain unmet. His sacrifice is admitted by Anglo-Catholic and Evangelical alike to be unique and unrepeatable. All this is solid gain. I suppose, there is hardly a priest of any learning within the Anglican Communion who would argue the old medieval dogma of Catholicism that in the eucharist the priest offers Christ for the sins of the living and the dead. It is now, thank God, universally recognized that Christ's priesthood is final and complete, and that His sacrifice of Himself upon the cross for man's forgiveness can neither be added to nor repeated. Thus Father Hebert asserts, 'the sacrificial action is not any sort of re-immolation of Christ, not a sacrifice additional to His one sacrifice, but a participation of it', and he strongly repudiates 'any idea that in the eucharist we offer a sacrifice to propitiate God'.[1] So far so good. It is difficult to see how any other view could ever have gained acceptance amongst any familiar with the argument of the Epistle to the Hebrews, with its reiteration of the finality of Christ's sacrifice and the sufficiency of His sacrifice (for example 7: 23–28; 9: 24–28; 10: 1–22, especially 10–14, 16–21). 'Christ thus abolishes all further human priesthood,' writes Prof. A. Richardson.[2]

One might go further and point out that any such priest would suffer from the same three defects which marred the efficacy of the old Jewish priesthood. In the first place, he would be a sinner, himself needing forgiveness, and therefore unable to procure it for others (Heb. 7: 26, 27). Secondly, he could not offer a sacrifice which is acceptable to God, for whom nothing is good enough but the total obedience of a life of utter love to Him (10: 4–10), and from whom sin makes a complete separation (Is. 59: 1, 2; Rom. 6: 23). That is why the sacrifice of Calvary, when Christ offered up His perfect, sinless life of love and obedience for us, and so broke down for ever the barrier caused by sin (Heb. 9: 12; 10: 12), needs and admits of no addition or repetition. And thirdly, of course, no other priest can create for man a permanent and satisfactory relationship with God, because he dies, whereas Jesus can always save those who come to God by Him, because the very

---

[1] In *Ways of Worship*, cited with approval in the *Lambeth Report* (1958), 2.85.
[2] *An Introduction to the Theology of the New Testament*, S.C.M. (1958), p. 201.

presence in heaven of the crucified and risen Saviour is the guarantee of their acceptance (7: 25; cf. 10: 12–14). No wonder, in view of all this, that the author of the Epistle to the Hebrews cries out in triumph, 'We have such an high priest' (8: 1).

2. *The Priesthood of all Christians and their Sacrifice*

The New Testament sees in the person, life, death and resurrection of Jesus the perfect way to God for all to take; He is the great high priest through whom we can approach God with every confidence (Heb. 10: 21 f.). It is hardly surprising, therefore, that we do not hear of any priestly caste or group within the Christian Church. And yet, of course, it *is* surprising; it is simply staggering in view of the background of these New Testament writers, steeped as they were in the priestly system of the Old Testament, that never once do they use the word *hiereus* of the Christian minister. The Aaronic analogy for their ministry lay obviously to hand. But they refused to use it. It is hard to overrate the significance of this point when we notice that they *did* use it *of the whole Christian community*! Just as the ideal of the Servant originally applied to the whole of Israel, but shrank and shrank until it was embodied in Jesus alone, and thenceforward belonged distinctively to His Body, the Church; so it was with priesthood. Originally the whole nation of Israel was called to be a nation of priests (Ex. 19: 6) to bring the Gentile world to God and represent God to the Gentile world. But Israel did not fulfil her function; neither did the Aaronic priesthood; neither did the high priest himself; it was only Jesus who brought God to men and brought men back to God. He is *the* priest *par excellence*. But now His people share His office. They cannot, to be sure, make sacrifice for sins; that expiatory part in the function of the Priest, as in that of the Servant, Christ has fulfilled alone, and once for all. But the other elements in the priestly role have devolved upon the whole Christian community without distinction. The Christian Church, in fact, realizes the ideal which the Jewish Church recognized but never achieved. For the Church *is* a nation of priests (Rev. 1: 6; I Pet. 2: 9; cf. Ex. 19: 6). What that means is expressed in three ways in the New Testament, in terms of access, mediation and offering.

In the first place, the priesthood common to all believers

carries with it unrestricted access to God. In the Old Testament this had been the prerogative of the priests, and supremely of the high priest. Only he could venture, and that but once a year and with sacrificial blood, into the Holy of Holies. Now the way into the holy presence of God has been made open once and for all, through the sacrifice of Christ. And now every believer has the priestly privilege of immediate access to God through Jesus (Rom. 5: 2; Eph. 2: 18; Heb. 4: 16; 10:19; I Pet. 3: 18). No other intermediary is either possible or necessary.

Secondly, priesthood in the Old Testament was mediatorial. The priest represented God to the people, when he declared to them God's will, and the people to God, when he interceded with Him on their behalf. Now the Christian Church is to bear this double responsibility. 'You are a chosen race, a royal priesthood, a holy nation, God's own people, that you may declare the wonderful deeds of Him who called you out of darkness into His marvellous light' (I Pet. 2: 9). It is the job of every member of the Church both to *go* into all the world and preach the Gospel to every creature, and to *pray* for that world to God (I Tim. 2: 1). This two-way mediation of evangelism and prayer is the solemn, lifelong calling of every Christian, and it is significant that these two activities are both spoken of as priestly ministries in the New Testament (Rom. 15: 16; Rev. 8: 3 ff.).

In the third place, the Church, and every Christian in it, inherits the priestly task of offering gifts and sacrifices to God (I Pet. 2: 5). Of course, for this had always been the task of the priest under the Old Testament (Heb. 8: 3). The sacrifices which are mentioned in the New Testament are the sacrifices of praise and thanksgiving (Heb. 13: 15), of faith (Phil. 2: 17), almsgiving (Acts 24: 17; Phil. 4: 18), a godly generous life (Heb. 13: 16), and supremely the sacrifice of ourselves, the yielding of our bodies as a thank-offering to God (Rom. 12: 1, 2).

Two things are noteworthy about this priestly work. In the first place, it belongs to every Christian, not to any ministerial group. In the second place, 'our offerings are not propitiations, for nothing that we could do could have turned away God's wrath. It is solely because of what God has done that we are able to approach Him and bring offerings in which He will take pleasure. It is because of Christ's one, true, effective sacrifice, offered once for all, that our unworthy oblation is possible.'[3]

3. The Priesthood of Ministers, and their Sacrifice

Priesthood is never associated with *presbyters* in the New Testament. Christian ministers are no more priests, and no less so, than any other members of Christ's priestly Body. The idea of a priestly ministerial caste came originally into Christianity from pagan sources,[4] and was furthered by analogies from Jewish practice. Even so, it was not until Cyprian in the middle of the third century that we find the word *hiereus* being regularly used of the Christian minister. Cyprian himself did much to transform the New Testament presbyter into the 'Catholic' priest.

Furthermore, the eucharist is never, in the New Testament, called a sacrifice, though, of course, Christ's death, which it displays, was *the* sacrifice for sins. But the holy communion is not seen as one of the many things we offer to God. It is something He offers to us; that is why it is called a sacrament of the *Gospel*. The primary movement in both the Gospel and its sacrament is from God to man, and not from man to God — a form of Pelagianism which has considerable currency today. It is significant that the Lambeth Report of 1958 quoted with approval these words of Dr. Hebert: 'The true celebrant is Christ the High Priest, and the Christian people are assembled as members of His Body to present before God His Sacrifice, and to be themselves offered up in sacrifice through their union with Him'; and the bishops themselves go on to say: 'We are partakers of the sacrifice of Christ (I Cor. 10: 16) . . . Christ with us offers us in Himself to God.' There is a great deal of truth in this eirenic statement, as there is in the following citations from a Roman Catholic writer, but there are unbiblical emphases in each. In speaking of the mass as a sacrifice, a characteristic exponent of the modern liturgical movement in the Roman Church writes:[5] 'At the mass Jesus does not die. The Risen Christ never dies again . . . but we are saved through His death. The Cross is the very source of our life.

[3] Richardson: *op. cit.*, p. 303.

[4] See Lightfoot: *op. cit.*, pp. 123 ff., Lindsay: *op. cit.*, p. 308, cf. Tertullian: *de Baptismo* 5.

[5] *Les Albums Liturgiques—La Messe*, Fleuret-Louvel, Paris, p. 9 (my translation from the French).

And it is the mass that presents it to us. For there are not two sacrifices, that of the Cross and that of the mass. There is the once-for-all sacrifice of Christ. . . . It is Jesus who does the offering; same Priest, same Victim, same Sacrifice.'

So far so good, as in the earlier part of Dr. Hebert's statement, which is, of course, influenced by current Roman thinking. But then we read on: 'It is not only Jesus who offers for us His Sacrifice to the Father, the whole Church joins with Him in making the offering. . . . It is the assured conviction of the Church when she celebrates mass that she offers the Sacrifice of Jesus. The Sacrifice is ours because it was offered for us. It is ours because at the mass we unite our sorrows, small though they be, with the great sufferings of Jesus. It is ours, because we present it in our turn.' I cannot find any great difference between this Roman Catholic statement and the position recommended by the Lambeth Conference. Both contain much that is helpful, but both, it seems, depart from Scripture at one or two significant points.

When it is suggested that the Church offers to God Christ's unique offering, this is something quite alien to the New Testament, which sees Christ as the One who made that sacrifice not *with* us but *for* us when He took the world's sin upon Himself once for all upon the cross, and then sat down in the place of honour and victory at God's right hand. It cannot be the case that He is now offering His sacrifice in the heavenly sanctuary, while the Church offers it on the earthly altar, as Moberly, Bicknell, Hicks and others suggest. For, according to the imagery of Hebrews, there is no altar in heaven any more than there was an altar in the Holy of Holies in the Jewish Tabernacle (Heb. 9: 24). As a Roman Catholic writer himself put it, 'the idea that Christ officiates before the throne of God by any sort of liturgical action or by any active pleading of His passion is nowhere to be found' (in Hebrews or in the rest of the New Testament for that matter). 'There is no heavenly sacrifice of Christ, but the living Priest holds all the power of His sacrifice in His living humanity.'[6] That is just the point. Jesus is not constantly offering to the Father His sacrifice once made. Chrysostom rightly says: 'Do not think, because you have heard that Jesus is a priest, that He is always offering sacrifice. He offered sacrifice once and for all,

⁶ W. Leonard: *The Authorship of the Epistle to the Hebrews* (1939), pp. 73, 75.

and thenceforward He sat down' (*Hom. in Heb.* 13: 8). He is now, in Richardson's phrase (*op. cit.*, p. 202), 'seated in the seat of the Vizier, not standing in the posture of the suppliant'.

But does the New Testament not say that Jesus is praying for His people (Rom. 8: 34; Heb. 7: 25)? It does, but a rare and significant word is used. It does not mean that He is asking for our acceptance, as though from a Father who is reluctant to grant it. For the Father has already accepted the sacrifice which Jesus made for sins, and the resurrection is the abiding proof of it (Rom. 4: 25). Indeed, the Father *shared in* the sacrifice of Calvary (II Cor. 5: 19). How should He need a reminder of it?[7] How should He need to have it pleaded? This doctrine of the heavenly sacrifice of Christ, invented to find room for a priestly offering by men in the eucharist, in fact drives a wedge between the attitude of the Father and the Son in our redemption. It gives us a flattering doctrine of eucharistic sacrifice at the expense of a Christian doctrine of God! Westcott saw long ago what the heavenly intercession of Christ did and did not mean: 'The modern conception of Christ pleading in heaven His passion, offering His blood on behalf of men, has no foundation in Hebrews. His glorified humanity is the eternal pledge of the absolute efficacy of His accomplished work. He pleads by His very presence on the Father's throne.'[8]

Our difficulties here are at least partly due to the ambiguities of language. Thus Christ does not *plead* His sacrifice, in the normal sense of the word, because it is already accepted; but He can properly be said to 'plead His sacrifice' if by that is meant that His presence as the Lamb once slain in the midst of the throne (Rev. 5: 6) is the silent plea for our acceptance. He does not *present* His sacrifice, if by that is meant constantly to offer to the Father the sacrifice of Calvary; but He may rightly be said to 'present' it (and so, indeed may we) if by that is meant to draw attention to the sacrifice once offered. It will be disastrous for ecumenical advance if some churchmen take fright at the language others are using, without

[7] This doctrine evoked John Knox's protest long ago: 'Is there any oblivion or forgetfulness fallen on God the Father? Hath He forgotten the death and passion of Jesus Christ, so that He needs to be brought in memory thereof by any mortal man?'

[8] *Hebrews*, Macmillan (1892), p. 230.

pausing to analyse whether such terms are necessarily to be construed in the most sinister way!

A further ambiguous phrase which causes great heart-burning is any talk of our 'uniting our sufferings' or 'joining our offerings' to those of Christ. This can so easily detract from the uniqueness of Christ's work. His sufferings were atoning; ours are not. His sacrifice removed the sin of the world; ours does not. The New Testament does not speak of our 'offering Christ' or 'presenting His sacrifice'; we do not associate ourselves and our offering of fitful obedience and thanksgiving with His offering which bore away the sin of the world. We are indeed 'partakers of the sacrifice of Christ', but partakers in the *benefits* that flow from that sacrifice, not in the *making* of it. Our offering of ourselves is not part of the offering of Christ, but a grateful response to His prior act.

All this is a most important emphasis which tends to be neglected today in a good deal of eucharistic discussion which verges on obscuring the distinction between the Saviour and the saved. Nevertheless there is a sense in which we share in sacrifice with Christ as well as responding to His initiative. It is most important both to recognize and to isolate this sense of sharing in the sacrifice of Christ.

If we talk about Christ's death as a sacrifice, we use Old Testament language. The Old Testament knew two different kinds of sacrifice; the sin offering, which came under divine displeasure, and the burnt offering, etc. which was a sweet-smelling savour and pleasing to God. The sacrifice of Christ fulfilled both these Old Testament types of offering. Viewed as a sin-offering, His sacrifice was utterly unique; we can only accept its benefit and respond to it in gratitude. Viewed as a burnt-offering it is unique indeed, in its perfection, but not in its character, for it is the pattern and ideal of our own self-offering (Eph. 5:2). In this sense we do share with Christ in His self-oblation. It is because Christ's sacrifice was at the same time both expiatory and dedicatory, whereas ours is only the latter, that the confusion arises. His atoning sacrifice is the *root* of our salvation; our responsive sacrifice of praise, thanksgiving and surrender is the *fruit* of it. The two must never be confused.

It is true that the Christians in the second and third centuries often spoke of the holy communion, as well as prayer, evangelism and so on, in sacrificial terms. But never did they suggest that our sacrifice is incorporated in Christ's. Instead they saw the eucharist as the fulfilment of the prophecy of Mal. 1 : 11 and of the Old Testament meal-offering. It was a 'sacrifice of thanksgiving' which the Church 'offers to God for having made the world and all that is in it for man's sake, and also for having set us free from evil'.[9] The eucharist was 'a sacrifice in the sense of a real offering to God of money, goods, devotion and prayer; it was not designed in any way to ensure the forgiveness of sins; and it was offered by the entire priestly body, that is the whole Church'.[10] As a Roman Catholic liturgiologist puts it: 'The Church is a priestly body to offer up spiritual sacrifices through Jesus Christ. I am sure that it is no accident that the primitive Church did not apply the term *hiereus* to either bishop or presbyter. It was applied in the first place to Christ. He is the priest, the high priest eternal. Secondly, they applied it to the assembly of Christians. . . . It was only in the third instance that *hiereus* and *sacerdos* were used of Christian ministers . . . they occupied an altogether different position from that of pagan priests or even the Old Testament priest.'[11] The 'altogether different position' that they occupied is defined in F. D. Maurice's distinction, taken over by Lightfoot, that the Christian priesthood is '*representative* without being *vicarial*'. That is to say, when a presbyter of the Church celebrates the communion, he is exercising the double representative function which we have seen to characterize the priesthood of all believers. He acts on behalf of God when in God's name he proclaims the Gospel of grace, and declares God's willingness to forgive the truly penitent. Again, he acts as Christ's representative when he utters the words and performs the actions with which Christ instituted the sacrament. He acts on behalf of men in leading the prayers and praises and presenting the offerings of the congregations. He is acting as a *representative*. He does not thereby take away the Christian layman's right of direct access to God, nor of assuring a penitent friend whom he has led to faith of God's certain pardon, nor his responsibility to offer his all to God and to proclaim to the unbelieving God's way of salvation. When the minister acts as God's mouthpiece, 'he

[9] Justin: *Dialogue* 41.
[10] E. M. B. Green in *Eucharistic Sacrifice*, ed. J. I. Packer (London, 1962), p. 77. The early patristic evidence is there surveyed.
[11] J. A. Jungmann: *The Early Liturgy*, D.L.T. (1960), pp. 17 f.

loes not interpose between God and man in such a way that
direct communion with God is superseded on the one hand,
or that his own mediation becomes indispensable on the other'.[12]
And when he acts as the mouthpiece of the congregation, as
'the delegate of a priestly race . . . here too his function cannot
be absolute and indispensable. It may be a general rule . . .
that the highest acts of congregational worship shall be performed through the principal officers of the congregation.
But an emergency may arise when . . . the layman will assume
functions which are otherwise restricted to the ordained
minister.'[13] Such is Lightfoot's conclusion of the whole matter.
I do not believe that any other can be derived from Holy
Scripture.

B. PRIESTHOOD AND SACRIFICE IN ANGLICAN TEACHING

Cranmer, the architect of the Prayer Book, has this to say of
the Christian priesthood: 'The difference between the priest
and the layman in this matter is only in ministration; that the
priest, as a common minister of the Church, doth minister and
distribute the Lord's Supper unto other, and other receive it
at his hand.'[14] Logically, therefore, he used 'priest' and
'minister' interchangeably in the Prayer Book. Of sacrifice, he
has this to say: 'One kind of sacrifice there is which is called
a propitiatory or merciful sacrifice, that is to say, such a
sacrifice as pacifieth God's wrath and indignation, and obtain-
eth mercy and forgiveness for all our sins. . . . And although
in the Old Testament there were certain sacrifices called by
that name, yet in very deed there is but one such sacrifice
whereby our sins be pardoned . . . which is the death of God's
Son, our Lord Jesus Christ; nor never was any other sacrifice
propitiatory at any time, nor never shall be. This is the honour
and glory of this our high priest, wherein he admitteth neither
partner not successor. . . . Another kind of sacrifice there is,
which doth not reconcile us to God, but is made of them which
be reconciled by Christ . . . to show ourselves thankful to
Him; and therefore they be called sacrifices of laud, praise
and thanksgiving. The first kind of sacrifice Christ offered to

[12] Lightfoot: *op. cit.*, p. 134.
[13] *Ibid.*
[14] *The Lord's Supper*, V.11.

God for us; the second kind we ourselves offer to God by Christ.'[15] Logically, therefore, he constructed the Communion Service in such a way that it would make this distinction perfectly plain. No mention of our sacrifice of 'ourselves, our souls and bodies' is made until after our reception of the elements which make real to us 'His one full, perfect and sufficient sacrifice for the sins of the whole world'. It is in order to maintain this vital distinction between Christ's sacrifice and ours, and not because of any innate conservatism, that evangelicals are anxious that the Prayer of Oblation should remain in the position in which Cranmer put it.

If this was the view of Cranmer, what of Hooker? 'I rather term the one sort [of clergy] *presbyters* than *priests*, because in a matter of so small moment I would not offend their ears to whom the name of priesthood is odious, though without cause.' (Hooker then explains the derivation of priest from *presbyteros*, but admits that it is commonly associated with sacrifice.) 'Seeing then', he continued, 'that sacrifice is now no part of the church ministry, how should the name of priesthood be thereunto applied? . . . Wherefore whether we call it a priesthood, a presbytership, or a ministry it skilleth not: although in truth the word *presbyter* doth seem more fit, and in propriety of speech more agreeable than *priest* with the drift of the whole Gospel of Jesus Christ.'[16]

It would be tedious to show how this view remained characteristic of the Church of England until the Oxford Movement. This has been superbly done by Professor Sykes.[17] It simply cannot be denied that at the Reformation the notion of a sacrificial priesthood was firmly repudiated. Indeed, at the ordination of a priest, the medieval habit of giving the man a patten and chalice as the emblem of his priestly office was significantly altered. From now on, he was given a Bible. It is hardly surprising, therefore, that Anglican orders are condemned by Rome because they lack the intention to make a man a priest in the sacrificial sense. The old priest has become the new presbyter. That is the position of the Church of England. Whatever the views of some of her members, a church's doctrine must be judged by her formularies. There is no doubt that the formularies of the Church of England, the

[15] *Op. cit.*, v.3.
[16] *Eccl. Pol.*, v.78.
[17] *Old Priest and New Presbyter*, C.U.P., 1956.

Bible, the Book of Common Prayer, and the Articles of Religion, do not favour the interpretation of priesthood and sacrifice advocated by 'Catholic' Christendom. Newman began the Oxford Movement convinced that he could, by subtle casuistry, reconcile the Articles with the Council of Trent. He later realized the dishonesty of such an attempt, and left the Anglican for the Roman fold.

The Church of England is comprehensive, and it is good that those with divergent theologies should live together in one Church (within the limits imposed by its formularies) and thereby show that Christian love and fellowship go deeper than theological differences. But those Anglicans who do not adopt Tractarian views of the ministry and sacraments have a right to ask that these comparatively recent intrusions into the historic ethos of Anglicanism should not be regarded as the quasi-official view of the Church. In particular, let there be an unequivocal recognition of those ministries of orthodox Christian communions which do not claim to stand within the apostolic succession.[18] To commend episcopacy, wrote the Bishop of Woolwich, 'not as the source and symbol of unity but as a gimmick for validating sacraments—this is what neither Presbyterians nor Methodists, nor any other non-

[18] There is one way in which we could, perhaps, help our friends in the reformed tradition to understand us at the present time. We could revert to the name *presbyter* for *priest*. The two reasons advanced by Hooker are more than ever relevant today; it would remove the offence from those to whom the name *priest* is odious, and it would bring us more into line with primitive church practice and the Gospel of Christ. It is difficult to see that the change would be offensive to any section within the Anglican Communion. The historically minded would be glad to see the undoubted linguistic and historical meaning of the word *priest* demonstrated in this way; it is astonishing how many people seem unaware that 'priest' is an English contraction of the word 'presbyter'. The High Churchman would remember that the Scottish Episcopalian Prayer Book of 1637 has *presbyter* for *priest* throughout; and undoubtedly that Book, influenced as it was by Laud, has a more 'Catholic' flavour than the Book of Common Prayer of 1662. Even the Roman Catholic Church retains vestiges of the primitive usage which for centuries they employed, when they call the priest's house the presbytery. And the ecumenically minded would note that *presbyter* is the title used in the Church of South India. The restoration of this, the most primitive name for the Christian ministry, might go a long way towards removing barriers to reunion. A golden opportunity to restore it was missed in the Report of the Anglican-Methodist Conversations, and the failure to do so very properly called forth the protest of the Dissentients (*Report*, p. 60).

episcopalian church will stand *or ought to stand*.[19] If our Church does adopt this intransigent attitude to other communions she will be denying her past history since the Reformation, and will be repudiating whatever claim she still retains to be the Church *of England*. It was not without reason that Dr. Alec Vidler in *The Times* (7 December 1961) asked if the Church of England were to remain the Catholic Church of the land, or to become an episcopalian sect? If sacerdotalism and an exclusive doctrine of apostolic succession ever become the doctrine of our church, that is precisely what it will become.

[19] Bishop J. A. T. Robinson's *On Being the Church in the World*, S.C.M. (1960), p. 105. The whole essay on Episcopacy and Intercommunion is an important and penetrating piece of work.

CHAPTER EIGHT

EPILOGUE

THERE have inevitably been many omissions in a short book of this nature.

There has not been room to say much about the making of a minister of the Gospel. It is usual to recognize three elements; the call of God, of which the candidate is assured (cf. Acts 26: 16–18), the approval of the congregation of Christian people recognizing the divine call (cf. Acts 6: 3, and I Tim. 3: 7), and the solemn commissioning and authorizing to this ministry by the imposition of hands with prayer (Acts 6: 6; I Tim. 4: 14; II Tim. 1: 6). To this one might add explicitly what is implicit in the first of these conditions, namely that the candidate must have a personal knowledge of God's mercy to himself, a sinner (I Tim. 1: 12–14). Without that he cannot proclaim the Gospel of God's mercy to others with any conviction; and he will not himself survive the pressing temptations and deep discouragements that make fruitless the ministry of many sincere men who, like the young Wesley, are well equipped for their ministry — except that they lack the prime essential, a personal relationship to their Lord.

There has not been room to say anything about training for the ministry. One who is at present engaged in this work cannot help being concerned at the present overemphasis on intellectual compared with practical preparation for the ministry. In particular, many men are ordained with little experience of youth work, less of preaching, and some with no experience at all of evangelism. The intellectual equipment of men who will have to hold down a regular ministry in a parish is clearly of great importance; so is the spiritual experience of living together as a Christian community in a theological college. But this is no substitute for practical experience of the work of the ministry such as would be gained by having a year of one's training as an assistant to an active vicar in a vital congregation. I was impressed in South Africa recently to learn that candidates for the Methodist ministry there normally have three years of experience as lay ministers before their academic training. There was, not unnaturally, a far greater maturity and understanding of the real needs of people among them than could be seen in the Anglican ordinands in that country, or in our own, for that matter.

Despite these and other omissions and shortcomings in this treatment of the Christian ministry, the factors here considered do seem to be of cardinal importance. We *must* take seriously the ministry of Jesus as a pattern for service rather than rule, for the function rather than the office of Ministry. We *must* talk less about what a layman can or cannot do, and more about what he is *called* to do within the Christian Body. We *must* think less in terms of hierarchy and more about the mutual relationships of different members of the Body of Christ.

As regards the threefold ministry, we must beware both of giving up a division of ministry which has eminent justification in Scripture, history and reason, and at the same time of compelling others to accept it on pain of excommunication; there was, we must recall, a variety of polity even within the New Testament Church, and yet this was not allowed to hinder their table-fellowship. It befits us rather to take seriously the threefold ministry whose excellencies we so loudly proclaim.

1. Let us, then, not attempt to commend episcopacy on the wrong grounds, but take the first steps towards a more biblical and primitive pattern of episcopacy by increasing the number of dioceses and decreasing the number of administrative tasks which a bishop is expected to fulfil, and thus restore to the bishop his proper function of being the chief pastor, overseer and teacher of his people.

2. Let us not attempt to commend the priesthood to non-conformists on grounds which are neither to be found in Scripture nor in the historic position of Anglicanism, but rather seek to recover the New Testament meaning of presbyter as a man who is the teacher[1] (II Tim. 4: 5; 2: 2; 1:13; I Tim. 3: 2; 4: 6, etc.), pastor (I Tim. 4: 12–5: 3; Tit. 1: 9, 10;

[1] In the Pastoral Epistles teaching, preaching, wrestling with the Word of God, commending it, defending it—all this is seen as the permanent duty of the presbyter. It is worth considering what sort of priority it is given today—and what fruit we reap in ignorance, false doctrine and apathy among Christian people.

2: 1–10) and leader (I Tim. 1: 18; 5: 21; I Thess. 5: 12) of his people; a man who can teach without dogmatizing and lead without domineering, a man who is prepared to suffer with them and for them, following the example of the Suffering Servant of the Lord (II Tim. 2: 3, 9, 12, 24; cf. I Cor. 4: 8–10).

3. Let us seek to recover the primitive diaconate in some relevant form instead of retaining it as a fossilized relic of bygone usefulness, a one-year probationary period for the priesthood. We bemoan the shortage of clergy, and hanker after an auxiliary ministry, while all the time the remedy is within our own hands, the weapon lies rusting in our own armoury. Let us ordain men to the diaconate for life, a diaconate which embraces and swallows up the post of lay-reader and catechist, yes, and that of lady worker as well. Let them be the chief assistants to the presbyter in every parish. Of course, they will continue with their secular job—St. Paul and Aquila and others did in the New Testament period (Acts 18:3; 20: 34), as did perhaps the majority of Christian ministers for the next three hundred years. In this way the presbyter will be relieved of much of the administrative and secretarial work which so largely hinders him doing the work for which he was ordained; he will be set free so that he can give himself to the task of building up the saints for the work of service. Furthermore, the yawning gulf between the clergyman and the man in the street will be to some extent bridged by these deacons who manifestly serve God both in the Church and in the world.

Above all this little book has sought to emphasize the pattern of the Servant for the ministry of the Church. It will require a tremendous reversal of our current attitudes, both on the part of the laity and of the clergy. The layman will need to get a new idea of the ministry. No longer will he be satisfied with responding from time to time to appeals to 'help the Church', by which, of course, we clergy mean the institution of which we are the hub. He will have to realize that the very reason the ordained ministry exists is to equip the ordinary Christian for his ministry in the world. The pattern of the Servant thus holds good for both laity and clergy. 'We must not be satisfied,' writes Professor A. T. Hanson, 'until it is quite natural for the ordinary Christian to approach his minister for advice or action with the request, "Won't you help the Church . . . ?"'[2]

[2] *The Church of the Servant*, p. 106.

It will require no less of a revolution in the attitude of the clergy if the pattern of the Servant ministry is to be realized among us. It is we clergy, with our prejudices, our dogmas, our talk of the validity and regularity of orders, that so often hinder the oneness of Christ's people. Of course, we must not sacrifice truth in the quest of unity, but so often it is not truth by prejudice that holds us up, doctrines and practices which we refuse to examine dispassionately in the light of Scripture. If we really took seriously the example of Jesus our Servant, and the Servant-status and function that He has bequeathed us, we would repent of proud and hierarchical attitudes adopted in the past, recognize each other's ministers as brethren in Christ, and co-operate forthwith in the work of the Kingdom of God. What an impetus for their own sacrificial service it would give to the people of God throughout the world, if they saw their leaders following in the path of the Servant! What progress it would mean for the Gospel of God if Christian leaders really behaved in this revolutionary way of their Founder, a way so contrary to the natural man that it could not fail to impress men with the power of this message which at last the Christians both preach *and live*! And what joy it would bring to the heart of the Saviour who on the last most solemn evening of His life gave this charge to His disciples: 'If I then, your Lord and Teacher, have washed your feet, you also ought to wash one another's feet. For I have given you an example, that you also should do as I have done to you. Truly, truly, I say to you, a servant is not greater than his master; nor is he who is sent greater than he who sent him. *If you know these things, blessed are you if you do them*'!

SELECT BIBLIOGRAPHY

H. S. Box, ed., *Priesthood*, S.P.C.K., 1937.
E. Brunner, *The Misunderstanding of the Church*, Lutterworth, 1952.
K. Carey, ed., *The Historic Episcopate*, Dacre Press, 1954.
G. Dix, *The Question of Anglican Orders*, Dacre Press, 1943.
Mgr. L. Duchesne, *Christian Worship*, S.P.C.K., 1903.
A. Ehrhardt, *The Apostolic Succession*, Lutterworth, 1953.
E. R. Fairweather, *Episcopacy Reasserted*, Mowbray, 1955.
E. R. Fairweather and R. F. Hettlinger, *Episcopacy and Reunion*, Mowbray, 1953.
P. T. Forsyth, *The Church and the Sacraments*, Longmans, 1917.
A. T. Hanson, *The Church of the Servant*, S.C.M. Press, 1961.
A. T. Hanson, *The Pioneer Ministry*, S.C.M. Press, 1961.
A. G. Hebert, *The Form of the Church*, Faber, 1944.
J. W. Hunkin, *Episcopal Ordination and Confirmation*, Heffer, 1929.
D. T. Jenkins, *The Nature of Catholicity*, Faber, 1942.
J. A. Jungmann, S. J., *The Early Liturgy*, D.L.T., 1960.
K. E. Kirk, ed., *The Apostolic Ministry*, Hodder and Stoughton, 1946.
T. M. Lindsay, *The Church and the Ministry in the Early Centuries*, Hodder and Stoughton, 1902.
J. B. Lightfoot, *The Christian Ministry*, Thynne & Jarvis, 1927.
T. W. Manson, *The Church's Ministry*, Hodder and Stoughton, 1948.
B. Minchin, *Every Man and his Ministry*, D.L.T., 1960.
R. C. Moberly, *Ministerial Priesthood*, John Murray, 1899.
L. Morris, *Ministers of God*, I.V.F., 1964.
C. F. D. Moule, *Worship in the New Testament*, Lutterworth, 1961.
Stephen Neill, *Anglicanism*, Pelican, 1958.
Stephen Neill, ed., *The Ministry of the Church*, The Canterbury Press, 1947.
L. Newbigin, *The Household of God*, S.C.M. Press, 1957.
J. I. Packer, ed., *Eucharistic Sacrifice*, Church Bookroom Press, 1962.
O. C. Quick, *The Christian Sacraments*, Nisbet, 1927.
A. Richardson, *An Introduction to the Theology of the New Testament*, S.C.M. Press, 1958.
C. Robinson, *The Ministry of Deaconesses*, Methuen, 1898.

W. Sanday, *The Conception of Priesthood*, Longmans, 1898.

E. Schweizer, *Church Order in the New Testament*, S.C.M. Press, 1961.

W. J. Sparrow Simpson, *The Ministry and the Eucharist*, S.P.C.K., 1942.

B. H. Streeter, *The Primitive Church*, Macmillan, 1929.

H. B. Swete, ed., *The Early History of the Church and Ministry*, Macmillan, 1918.

N. Sykes, *Old Priest and New Presbyter*, Cambridge University Press, 1956.

N. Sykes, *The Church of England and Non-Episcopal Churches in the Sixteenth and Seventeenth Centuries*, S.P.C.K., 1948.

T. F. Torrance, *Royal Priesthood*, S.J.T. Occasional Papers, 1955.

W. Tulfer, *The Office of a Bishop*, D.L.T., 1962.

Timothy Ware, *The Orthodox Church*, Penguin, 1963.

R. Whateley, *Apostolic Succession Considered*, Longmans, 1912.

H. J. Wotherspoon and J. M. Kirkpatrick, *A Manual of Church Doctrine according to the Church of Scotland*, revised and enlarged by T. F. Torrance and R. Selby Wright, Oxford University Press, 1960.

Catholicity, Dacre Press, 1947.

The Catholicity of Protestantism, Lutterworth, 1950.

Conversations between the Church of England and the Methodist Church: a Report, Church Information Office and Epworth Press, 1963.

The Fulness of Christ, S.P.C.K., 1950.